D1736312

How Do We Get the Graduates We Want?

How Do We Get the Graduates We Want?

A View from the Firing Lines

Edited by
Lewis C. Solmon *and*
Katherine Nouri Hughes

PRAEGER

New York
Westport, Connecticut
London

Library of Congress Cataloging-in-Publication Data

How do we get the graduates we want? : a view from the firing lines /
  edited by Lewis C. Solmon and Katherine Nouri Hughes.
    p. cm.
  Includes bibliographical references (p.) and index.
  ISBN 0-275-94272-4 (alk. paper)
  1. Education—United States—Aims and objectives. 2. High school
graduates—United States. I. Solmon, Lewis C. II. Hughes,
Katherine Nouri.
  LA217.2.H68 1992
  370'.973—dc20   92-7

British Library Cataloguing in Publication Data is available.

Library of Congress Catalog Card Number: 92-7
ISBN: 0-275-94272-4

First published in 1992

Praeger Publishers, One Madison Avenue, New York, NY 10010
An imprint of Greenwood Publishing Group, Inc.

Printed in the United States of America

The paper used in this book complies with the
Permanent Paper Standard issued by the National
Information Standards Organization (Z39.48-1984).

10 9 8 7 6 5 4 3 2 1

CONTENTS

ACKNOWLEDGMENTS

The editors gratefully acknowledge the invaluable contributions of several participants in the writing and production of this monograph. Dr. Cheryl Fagnano, in addition to being coauthor of the chapter on collaboration, provided much of the foundation for the final chapter, *"Additional Ideas on How to Get the Graduates We Want,"* with her extensive research. Dr. Fagnano also contributed greatly to the organization of the volume and to the design of the conference that led up to it. Mr. Lawrence Lesser, production director of the Foundations of the Milken Families, with the help of his staff members, David Archer and Doug Wilson, provided the technical expertise for getting the manuscript into publishable form. Christine Carrillo Miner, whose word-processing expertise is exceeded only by her patience, piloted one draft of this study into the next. She supervised the production of this book and dealt patiently with all the contributors. Patty Lacy provided valuable word-processing assistance for the final draft. Judy Selhorst, our copy editor, and Cristina Haley, who proofread the manuscript and produced the index, made invaluable contributions by turning a typed manuscript into a book. Finally, we would like to thank Apple Computers for lending the very substantial hardware and software that allowed for the recording of the retreat's workshop and also for the valuable loan of Apple consultants Ann Rivera and Keith Ramée, among many others. At times during the retreat Apple had more than a dozen staff assisting us. Most important, we would like to thank the 200 Award Winners and many visitors at the retreat whose ideas are reflected in what follows.

PREFACE

Lowell Milken

Conjecture about today's students and tomorrow's graduates — about who they are and what they should be like — issues from nearly every quarter. A key constituency from whom — through no fault of their own — all too little has been heard is America's educators. They have much to tell us, and this report provides an opportunity for some of the best of them to voice their ideas. *How Do We Get the Graduates We Want?* is based on the findings of an annual three-day retreat that is itself the culmination of the Foundations of the Milken Families' cornerstone effort: The Milken Family Foundation National Educator Award Program.

In 1981 my brother and I conceived an educator award program based on the belief that the most effective way to address the crisis in education is to focus on the needs and the resources of educators — and, specifically, to provide strong motivation for young men and women to enter and strengthen the profession. Among our early initiatives in the field of education were a number of programs specifically geared to the needs of educators. These included teacher incentive grant programs which provide curriculum, travel and study grants, salary supplement programs, and, most significantly, an award program, established in 1986. The aims of the Educator Award Program were to provide significant financial recognition for exemplary educators, to celebrate their commitment and accomplishment publicly, and, by means of this recognition, to encourage other young men and women of talent to enter the profession.

In 1987 the Milken Family Educator Award Program offered its first round of individual $25,000 awards in California to 12 men and women manifestly dedicated to excellence and creativity in education. From that first Educator Award celebration has grown the National Educator Award Program, now established in 15 states and still expanding. Including the 1991 Awards, the Program has honored 312 educators.

As my brother Mike noted of the inception and development of the Educator Award Program: "When we first developed the teacher incentive awards in the early 1980s, one of the things we hoped to do was communicate to teachers and educators that their efforts were not in vain; that their dedication and talent were recognized and appreciated in a very concrete way. As the Awards have evolved over the years, it has become clear that we honor not only individuals, but an entire community."

The Foundations of the Milken Families themselves were established in 1982 with a primary aim of improving our system of education — in our view, this country's single most important profession. The heart of the Foundations' mission has always been to help provide individual people of every age with the means and the will to help themselves and those around them lead productive, gratifying lives. No profession is more central to this effort than education. This is why we support well over 150 educational programs and organizations, ranging from curricular improvement programs and antiprejudice instruction to parent involvement efforts and a range of mentoring projects.

Notwithstanding these and other commendable programs, the complex and onerous burden that has been thrust upon the field of education and upon its practitioners has made it impossible to aid, improve, or refine our system of education without becoming engaged in other areas of human endeavor. How can we address the needs of a kindergartner who was born addicted to crack, for example, if we don't address the predicament of his teenage mother? How can we expect children to bring a basic sense of well-being to school when, for the last four years, one-fourth of them have been living in poverty? How do we teach a seventh grader kindness and respect if she has no home and both parents are effectively oblivious to her existence? And how are we supposed to find a decent job for a high school senior who has been promoted every year despite his functional illiteracy in both the languages he speaks?

These are the kinds of questions America's educators are asking every day. They are also the kinds of questions to which many of them have found creative and workable solutions. But neither the most brilliant theory nor the hardest-won experience will benefit the profession or the children it serves if it is not heard or made known. One of the chief reasons the Foundation established the National Educator Awards Retreat was precisely to respond to this need. The National Educator Awards Retreat is an annual three-day symposium that brings together award recipients past and present to discuss specific professional issues and to exchange with those gathered, including hundreds of topflight educators, the ideas and lessons they know have *worked*.

Given the dizzying pace of technological growth, the rapid globalization of commerce and industry, the fragmentation of the American family, and the fast-changing demographic composition of this country, the retreat's professional issues are as far-flung as determining and inculcating values, forging ongoing partnerships with other sectors, and meeting the complex needs of an increasingly diverse student population. They are also as rudimentary as the need to align what goes on in the classroom with what goes on in the "real world," for we can no longer afford to live with the illusion that the two are different.

These themes and many others addressed at the 1991 retreat accord with the overall enterprise of the Foundations. Because our core commitment is to education, and because our system of education does not exist in a social vacuum, our funding activities extend to the three areas we believe most directly affect American education generally and students and educators specifically: community services, health care and medical research, and human welfare. The concerns of these areas do more than overlap with the concerns of education; each is also a field that respects the integrity of the individual, recognizes people's essential needs, and lends itself to the development of their potential — attributes making these areas especially hospitable to our mission.

The most effective way to pull the giant strands of our future together is through education, in classrooms, and, most especially, by means of educators. Many of the ideas and the hard-earned experience of some of the best of our educators are recorded in the report that follows. We are proud of these men and women, and proud to celebrate their achievements. At least as important is the pride they take in themselves, as teachers and principals and administrators — as those who every day are proving that the future belongs to the educated.

How Do We Get the Graduates We Want?

INTRODUCTION

Lewis C. Solmon

For three days every March, the Milken Family Foundation National Educator Awards Retreat offers hundreds of our nation's most creative and talented educational practitioners the one, and perhaps the only, thing that they all agree they want: time. This is not leisure time, or even time to hone their already considerable teaching or administrative skills, but rather time to reflect on and then discuss what they have learned as working educators. They listen to some of our nation's most eminent educational scholars and powerful policymakers, and then they share with these people their own hard-won wisdom, born of years of professional training and experience. This book is a chronicle of how this time was spent during the 1991 retreat.

This year's retreat focused upon two related questions: What do we want our graduates to be like, and how do we get the graduates we want? These topics were chosen by the award winners themselves because they represent the basics of what practitioners are about: preparing students for their futures. Under these headings, specific areas of concern were addressed:

1. The moral and ethical development of our children.
2. Meeting the needs of diverse students.
3. Attracting, preparing, and retaining high-quality teachers.
4. School structure and restructuring.
5. Assessing effective school processes.
6. School, business, and university collaborations.

The retreat was organized to increase participants' opportunities to contribute to the discourse. Naturally, everyone had something to contribute, and while there was much ground for agreement, there was considerable room for enlivened debate as well. To set the stage for the two days' discussions, William Bennett, former secretary of education, and Arthur Levine of Harvard University offered opening addresses on the topic, "What do we want our graduates to be like?" Drs. Bennett and Levine were the ideal pair to open these deliberations. Dr. Bennett is a well-known and outspoken conservative, while Dr. Levine is an eloquent and scholarly voice of liberalism. Both of them, like our Award recipients themselves, are passionately devoted to ensuring a high-quality education for every child.

Following the opening comments, the award recipients were given time to respond to the presenters in a question-and-answer session. Four of the participating state superintendents of education then presented counterpoints to Drs. Levine and Bennett. The remainder of the first day was spent in intense small group discussions as the 200 teachers and administrators, representing every quadrant of the country and every disciplinary perspective, identified the types of graduates they hoped to produce.

Day 2 was devoted to the specifics of how to get the graduates we want. The deans of five Los Angeles-area schools of education were each invited to preside over the discussion of one of the subtopics. They, in turn, invited various scholars, community leaders, and policymakers to serve as additional resources for the topics. In these "how-to" sessions, perhaps more than at any other time during the retreat, the diversity, intensity, and commitment of the award winners were evident. Here reasonable men and women questioned, confronted contradictions, disagreed, and, ultimately, worked together to achieve one of their profession's most important goals: identifying ways to educate all our children more effectively.

What follows are not the theories of scholars, the bottom-line "realities" of businessmen, or the compromises of politicians. Presented on these pages are the concerns and thoughts of working teachers and administrators. These are the professionals who go into American schools and classrooms each day to listen when we often don't, to discipline when we often haven't, and to teach what we often can't. The voices you will hear are as diverse as the students they teach. Consider the following sentiments expressed by award recipients:

- Schools can and must teach values, but whose values?
- Schools must expand their horizons to include a more diverse curriculum, but if the United States is to remain a nation, our schools must teach a common heritage!
- Teaching is an occupation that features low wages, poor working conditions, waning professional prestige, declining public support, and few opportunities for exercise of professional judgment, yet we want — nay, we expect — some of our best and brightest students to become teachers.
- Who has the authority to structure a school day — the district, the school principal, the teacher?
- Norm-referenced tests provide a measure of teachers' success — data from standardized, multiple-choice tests allow us to understand only a portion of what children know.

- We need and want more involvement from the business community in our schools — yet there is some irony in corporations offering management "expertise" to schools even as they seek new keys to dealing with their own declining productivity and increasing international competition.

These are diverse views, certainly — but they are ideas held together by a common understanding of the place of education in our society, of the need for excellence, and of a commitment to American's future — our children.

The final chapter of this report is intended to serve as both summary and preface. Summary, because much of the chapter is based on the views from the how-to sessions reported in the chapters that precede it. Preface, because this retreat is not the end but the beginning for the National Educator Award recipients, who, as a group, now have the opportunity to add their voices to the public discourse on education. Thus, while I must take full responsibility for what is included in Chapter 12, much of it is informed by my public and private conversations with many of the retreat participants and is intended to provide intellectual grist for what are ongoing discussions.

For each of the how-to sessions, I have raised questions that in the time allotted at the retreat may have been only skimmed over (or merely implied) and left to wait for another time. But these are questions and concerns that I know the retreat participants wish to explore further. This final chapter is intended to point us in a clear direction for these future explorations. In the "Values" section, for example, the question is posed: If schools are to assume more responsibility for, and spend more time on, formally teaching values and ethics, which responsibilities of the schools must be sacrificed to find that extra time? With regard to meeting the needs of minority children, it is suggested that while we must provide a common heritage for all our children, there is a differential between the problems of poverty and the demand for diversity. Teachers are fervently implored to address the issues of merit pay and of their own accountability when they assume the increased responsibility inherent in school restructuring. As for assessment, it is clear that new approaches are called for, but what will be the costs, both in dollars and in the amount of time students must spend away from the classroom? Moreover, are we willing to pay these costs? And can any discussion of assessment be complete without consideration of competency testing for teachers? Finally, a word of caution on collaborations: Is the likelihood of their success dependent upon the fiscal health of the general economy, and, if they are dependent on such a variable, what kinds of collaborations do we really want?

In this economist's view, any discussion of school improvement must take into account the need for cost-benefit analysis. There are trade-offs to be made among student outcomes, among policy alternatives, and among ways to deploy increasingly limited resources. This book initiates the discussion of the choices educational practitioners would like us to make.

When this report was first planned, we anticipated an unprecedented document of practitioners' views of school reform. What follows is just that — but the perspectives presented go beyond those expressed by many of the exemplary practitioners at the retreat.

The two keynote speakers, one a policymaker at the federal level and the other a university professor and administrator, present their own perspectives. One editor has prepared a concluding chapter that provides something of a counterpoint to the practitioners' views. Even the deans' chapters summarizing participants' comments are affected by the deans' own values and points of view. We did, however, provide a representative group of award recipients the opportunity to add to the deans' chapters.

It is likely that some of the retreat's educators will disagree with at least some of what follows, but we feel that the broader perspective herein presented outweighs even the possibility of some recipients' desiring disclaimers. All of the alternative views, it should be noted are derived from reactions to the insights of the practitioners.

PART I

WHAT DO WE WANT
OUR GRADUATES TO BE LIKE?

THE GRADUATES WE WANT:
WHO THEY ARE AND HOW WE GET THEM

1

Arthur Levine

In recent years, there has been a rising level of criticism about the students coming to college. The criticism has concerned the facts that the proportion of minorities has decreased, particularly black males; that students' standardized test scores have dropped precipitously, with only slight recovery in recent years; that student abilities in basic skills — reading, writing, and arithmetic — have diminished; that students' mastery of advanced skills has fallen behind that of students in other industrialized nations; that students' general knowledge in key areas such as history and geography, has declined, with students unable to locate countries on the globe or historical events within a century; that business and industry complain that high school graduates are incompetent at fundamental work skills; that students are more career oriented, more materially driven, more civically detached, and more ethically uncertain than their predecessors of a decade and a half ago.

These are not the high school graduates we want. There is a widespread feeling that students used to be much better, and so were the schools that educated them. There is a belief that the American educational system, once the envy of the world, is failing. The United States has lost or, worse yet, let slip through its fingers a golden age in education. The only small source of disagreement in this analysis is about when and why the golden age ended.

Allan Bloom, a professor at the University of Chicago and one of the most visible and vocal critics of U.S. education in recent years, says the decline occurred in the 1960s. He attributes it to the cultural relativism of the era. But Robert Hutchins, former president of the University of Chicago, says the golden age ended even earlier. He chalks it up to the rise of professional schools — business, librarianship, diplomacy, education, and the rest — around the turn of the century. And economist Thorstein Veblen has said that the loss occurred just after the Civil War, with the adoption of the free elective system in education, which eliminated the required classical curriculum.

The faculty of Yale in 1828 blamed educational decline on contemporary reformers who were too focused on job preparation. Cardinal Newman of the University of Dublin cast responsibility at the feet of John Locke and his peers, for their liberal attitudes toward society. Dionysus of Halicanarsus in the first century B.C. blamed it on the Greeks for fostering premature specialization. My own personal choice is Plato, who one day leaned over to a student and said, "Get your requirements out of the way."

My point is this: In the United States we speak of social problems always as crises, as Tocqueville wrote long ago. Intrinsic to a crisis is a nostalgically remembered past — a golden age gone by. The fact of the matter is that we have not lost a golden era in education. None ever existed. But there are problems, very real problems, in American education. We are not getting the graduates any of us want.

The nation's reaction to these problems has been unfortunate. As the human and social toll of recent years has become apparent — declining educational achievement, decreasing global competitiveness, a troubled economy, stubborn and rising levels of poverty — there has been a desperate rush to find someone to blame. This is a historic curiosity of American life — we ask who did it before we ask what happened. The general conclusion has been that the schools are to blame. A sea of reports and an ocean of recommendations have confirmed the verdict.

But this conclusion doesn't seem to fit with the schools I've visited or most of the schools in which you work. When the first reports on the decline of the U.S. schools were published in the early 1980s, I was president of a small liberal arts college. Like many college presidents, I was disappointed in the quality of my institution's applicants. I arranged to spend a week at the most troubled high school in my local area, and enrolled in all the classes and activities a senior would take.

Lawrence High School suffers from all the problems that face today's schools — high dropout rates, too many teen pregnancies, low test scores, drugs, skyrocketing student and faculty turnover, and periodic violence. I expected to find a school in which teaching was poor and learning was meager, but that is not what I found at all. I found a school working hard to cope with very real, very large, and very complex and tenacious problems, none of its own making.

A number of the teachers I met could not afford to live on their teaching salaries and worked second, and occasionally third, jobs. A number were actively looking for new positions. School administrators told horror stories about losing faculty in science and math to industry. Bilingual teachers were impossible to hold. Two young faculty members, who loved their jobs, told me their parents opposed their choice of a teaching career and college counselors had told them they were too good to become teachers. Today the average annual teacher's salary in the United States is less than $29,000.

I attended classes where students had to share textbooks because there were not enough to go around. As a result, homework could be assigned only every other night. I was in a Spanish class in which the instructor was forced to teach Spanish to students learning a new language and English to Spanish-speaking students simultaneously. I saw basic skills classes with 30 and 40 students.

I met with students who were unlike the students I went to school with. I saw a youngster who enrolled in the middle of the term. He could not speak English, he was illiterate in his native Spanish, and he was going blind. I met a young woman on the lunch line. I asked her what she did when she was not in school. She worked in a restaurant from 3 until 11 p.m., Monday through Friday, and all weekend, as a manager. She was just a young girl and small in stature. I impulsively asked who would hire her as a manager, and she said her husband. Full-time school, full-time job, and a husband. In a typical year, 30 percent of the student body turns over at Lawrence High School.

Today, a majority of high school students work. At Lawrence, many work long hours, and discussion among students focuses far more on jobs than on any academic issue. Television, dating, drugs, family problems, and an endlessly diverting neighborhood make school far less important to today's Lawrence students than it was to their predecessors.

Churches, parents, and traditional youth groups have also diminished in importance. At Lawrence I met a young woman who had not been in school for several days. When I asked why, she said her sister was sick and her mother worked. Someone had to stay home and watch her sibling. More recently, I met a chronic truant who never came to school on Thursdays. I asked him why. Thursday was the day his brothers got the winter coats, he said. I visited an elementary school where the principal told me a kindergartner had brought drug works to school for "show and tell." It was just what the student found at home. I visited a Parent-Teacher Association meeting — three parents showed up. Today schools are facing the decline of the family, rising poverty, changing demographics, a drug explosion, and a lack of parental support.

What my visit to Lawrence says to me is that the schools are not the villains. They are the victims. While every school in the United States is not Lawrence High School (thank heaven!), all have been victims of an age of transition, a time of unprecedented social change — economic, demographic, social, global, and technological. Let's consider the barrage of changes.

We live in an economy that is turbulent and in transition. Our nation is moving from an industrial to a service base. Old industries are dying; new industries are being born. Unemployment is rising. Debt is growing. Banking is deeply troubled. The structure of jobs is changing, with an increasing number of positions requiring an increasing amount of education, while those requiring less education are disappearing. The nation is becoming less competitive in a global economy.

Consider demographics: The number of young people is decreasing as older populations grow. The proportion of whites is declining as the proportion of people of color rises. The percentage of poor is increasing as the middle class diminishes. The populations of the Northeast and Midwest are shrinking as the West and South expand.

Socially, the family is declining, women's roles are changing, drugs are becoming epidemic in our cities, violence is rising, organized religion is on the decline, poverty is spreading, and teenage pregnancies produce enough children to replace Boston annually.

Globally, the position of the United States is being transformed. We are inextricably intertwined in a global society, a dramatically shifting global society at that. We have learned painfully that our gas pumps are tied to the Middle East. We have seen auto production in Japan cost jobs in Detroit. We have watched as the inability of Third World countries to pay their debt has caused shock waves from New York to London to Tokyo.

And technologically, we are entering a brave new world. My grandmother was born before the airplane was invented. My daughter was born after man landed on the moon. I think about all the things that are everyday parts of our lives that were not a few years ago — fax, word processing, VCRs, cable television, computers, microwaves, ATMs. More and more, faster and faster.

Change of this magnitude is rare. The last time it occurred in this country was nearly 150 years ago, during the Industrial Revolution. However, when broad-scale change does occur, one of the consequences is that every social institution in the society, schools included, gets left behind. A period of readjustment is required. Time is needed.

Sorting out the changes as they occur, even making sense of them, is a guessing game. What is cause? What is effect? What is temporary? What is permanent? Will this period ultimately be called the great demographic transition, the economic shift, the technological revolution, the global transformation, or perhaps a combination of these? Jane Bryant Quinn says that if you are not confused about what is going on today, you don't understand it.

Unfortunately, we name periods of such rapid and widespread change only in retrospect. The name Industrial Revolution didn't stick until 70 years after the changes began. For the people living through these periods, they are times of confusion, loss, uncertainty, floundering, and flailing. For the schools, they are periods of disorientation, times in which the nation is more certain about the length of an education than its purpose, content, or performance. They are periods of searching self-examination for the schools, times in which reports are written criticizing the condition of education. In every era the reports have been the same, their content constant. Perennially we lament the loss of quality, the decline of discipline, the rise of disorder, the poverty of teaching and the teaching corps, reduced standards, and the diminishing excellence of our graduates.

Innovation and experimentation follow: new subject matters, new curricula, new pedagogies, new technologies, new methods of organization. As a consensus is reached regarding the appropriate purpose and design of education, the extraordinary climate for innovation wanes.

Our schools have always moved toward the changing society by a process of successive approximations. To do this consciously and creatively should be the mission of the schools today. We need graduates who are adept at living in a society in transition. Let's consider what this means for the graduates we want.

Historically, the United States has always — from the time of our earliest schools — asked for the same four things in graduates: basic skills, knowledge about our common heritage and the society in which we live, good character, and preparation for work or further study. Our definitions of these four attributes have changed over time, however. In the beginning, when we spoke of *basic skills,* we referred to graduates who knew the "3 Rs." *Common knowledge* meant knowledge of the Bible and the classics, often in their original languages. *Good character* meant having the traits of a Christian gentleman. And *preparation for work* meant work in agriculture — later, in manufacturing — and college for very few.

As the country grew older, the economy advanced, social realities became more complex, and knowledge increased, our definitions of the four areas expanded. The "3 Rs" were not enough — we wanted higher-order intellectual skills as well, including analysis, synthesis, and problem solving. The body of knowledge that students needed to master multiplied. Arithmetic, for example, became algebra, geometry, and trigonometry. The Christian virtues remained essential, but America extended their teaching to women, minorities, and other religious groups as well as into new civic, health, global, technological, environmental, and economic realities. Preparation for work came to mean educating students for a multiplying number of educational possibilities and jobs. Agriculture and manufacturing expanded to include the trades, blue-collar, white-collar, technical, and professional work.

The historical pattern has been one of accretion, adding more and more to what we expect of our graduates, rarely subtracting from the list. Perhaps this is why the renowned nineteenth-century medieval historian Hastings Rashdall wrote that the half-educated man of today knows a great deal more true and useful knowledge than did the medieval doctor of divinity. Perhaps this is why schooling increased from eight years to twelve years, largely in the past century.

In recent years, we have found ourselves with two big problems with regard to our graduates. The first is a rising level of uncertainty about what skills, knowledge, character, and career preparation students most need in a changing world. The second is that we are living in two worlds simultaneously — adding the new dimensions to the desired characteristics and maintaining the old. In attempting to balance both, we have produced too many graduates who have come through schooling with neither. They lack the historically required skills, knowledge, character, and career preparation, and they lack the attributes they require for living today and tomorrow. I would suggest we have two agendas for our graduates: The first is more, and the second is better.

When I speak of more, what I mean is more students graduating from high school and going on to college, particularly people of color. Today almost 30 percent of all youngsters drop out before completing high school. In our country's four largest states, the rate climbs to 38 percent. And in the nation's capital, it rises to 42 percent. For minorities and the poor, the results are even worse.

Only a bare majority of Hispanics and fewer than two out of three blacks are graduating from high school.

In the last several years, the schools have made small increases in Hispanic and black retention rates, but the colleges have lost ground. There is a long way to go, longer for higher education. However, results at a number of schools show we already know how to improve graduation rates significantly at both levels. We only need do it.

At the same time, however, it is important to recognize that the schools cannot reverse dropout rates alone. I have been studying, even living for a short while, in a low-income housing project. I have talked with the children there, ages 6 to 15 primarily. I have asked them what they want to be when they grow up. Their plans are modest — a fire fighter, a secretary, a plumber, a truck driver. When I ask, "Will you get to do these things?" the answer is a shrug or a no.

When I ask, "If you could go as far as you want in school, how far would you go?" the response is tenth grade, followed distantly by twelfth. When I ask, "Do you know anyone who has ever attended college?" the answer is no. "Do you know anyone who has ever graduated from high school?" They say friends of relatives and relatives of friends — no one in their immediate lives. Schooling for them is a distant reality.

For many, school is too late. What these youngsters need is early, comprehensive intervention in their lives. They need pre- and postnatal care. Many are preemies who never catch up with their peers. Their parents need parenting education, with emphasis on nutrition and nurturing, as many are only children themselves and know nothing about bringing up youngsters. They need strong and rich day-care centers and preschools to overcome the language and learning difficulties that will cause many of these young people to fall a grade behind by the third year of school. They need pregnancy prevention programs, because each time a teen has a child, we witness the potential for two generations of poverty: the 15-year-old mother who may be poor for the rest of her life and the child who has a 70 percent chance of living below the poverty line. And finally, they need drug abuse prevention programs. The children I talk with are the only group in America we have succeeded in teaching the metric system. They know grams and kilograms at an early age.

The schools cannot do all of this. What is required is government action. Most of the activities I've suggested have an immediate payback — savings in health care, prison, welfare, and education costs. We are going to pay the price for these young people, in one fashion or another, either when they are young and healthy, or later when their lives are broken. Why not do it when it can make the most difference?

What I have suggested is a good investment. In fact, it is the best investment I can imagine, if we are serious about producing more high school and college graduates.

Hand in hand with more graduates, however, is the need for better-prepared graduates. Toward this end I would suggest that we update the four historic goals for our graduates. Let us preserve what has been important in the past and augment it with what is needed in the present.

With regard to skills, we need to produce graduates who have learned basic and higher-order intellectual skills. But I would propose, for this generation that will live in an age of transition, that we augment their skills with the "3 Cs": critical thinking (the ability to question and evaluate the tidal wave of information we encounter each day), creativity (the ability to imagine in a time in which old questions and answers are growing tired), and continuous learning (the ability to educate oneself autonomously, as the half-life of knowledge grows shorter and shorter).

With regard to knowledge about our common heritage and civilization, we have developed a curriculum over the years that includes language, literature, history, mathematics, civics, science, the arts, and physical well-being. The challenge, and the pressing need, for all of us is to ground students in the basic principles and teach them how to think in each of these areas. This has always been the challenge. But today there is another challenge as well, and that is to expand the perspective of our graduates from their traditional Western focus to the international understanding critical for survival in an increasingly global society. Additionally, students need to know more about domestic diversity if they are to live in a country that is growing more diverse in population every day.

With regard to values, four very large needs stand out for today's young people. One is hope. My research shows that today's students have grown cynical at an early age. They have few heroes. They believe most people only look out for number one. They are far more optimistic about their personal futures than about our collective future. They need hope, not the dewy-eyed Pollyannaish type, but the kind that gives people the fortitude to go on and build a better tomorrow.

Another need is self-efficacy — the belief that what one does is consequential and makes a difference. Students don't have this now. A feeling of impotence is widespread. Few believe they can make a difference.

Also critical is responsibility — a recognition of being part of a larger community and being obligated to others. This is low in many of the students we have studied. Senses of victimization and entitlement are common. Until recently, altruism has been minimal and materialism high. Young people share a *"Titanic* ethic" — a feeling that the United States or the world is going down and, as long as they are forced to ride on a doomed ship, they owe it to themselves to make the voyage as luxurious as possible and go first class.

The final item in the list of needs is empathy, or tolerance. I am not speaking of the uncritical acceptance of all change, the 1960s attitude of let a hundred flowers bloom. I am talking about the ability of students to live with change and diversity, to live with each other. In recent interviews with college students, I've found a growing inability among diverse young people to talk with one another, and a rising level of anger among them.

Preparation for the future itself may be the most difficult challenge facing the schools. In essence, we have to ready students for jobs and careers that may not exist now, jobs and careers that will require more, not less, education. We have to prepare them for lives in which the U.S. Department of Labor says on average they will have seven different careers. We have to start them off on a road that none of us has traveled, in which the combinations of work, home, civic life, and education may be differently construed and mixed than in the past. This raises large questions about the adequacy of existing approaches to tracking, and whether current tracks and the futures associated with them make career sense. We need to think about offering more formal curricular approaches to career, education, and life planning, particularly for young people with little personal or family experience with extended education.

This is a very large agenda. For our nation to increase simultaneously the number and the quality of our graduates, several changes will be essential. First, the emphasis in education will have to shift from processes to outcomes. Our students are too heterogeneous, transfer too often among too many school systems, and learn in too many different ways for us to continue to focus primarily upon common processes — Carnegie units, 50-minute hours, 180-day years, age grouping, and the rest. The real need is to achieve commonality of outcomes for all students, with a multiplicity of ways of accomplishing this.

Second, schools need freedom and accountability. Each school must be able to shape a program for achieving its mission, and the school and its principal must be held accountable for the results.

Third, schools need time. The next few years will bring pressure for quick fixes. This will come in varying degrees from business, government, the press, and the public. Not long ago, one of the biggest corporate philanthropists in school reform came to see me. He asked how long it would take to get our schools back in order. He said he thought that five years should be more than enough. If the auto industry could do it in five years, so could the schools. I explained that the auto industry had not turned itself around, and that the products that come out of the schools take 12 years to produce, in contrast to a few years for a new line of cars. I said education now recognizes that there are serious problems, but we are uncertain of the solutions. A plethora of reform efforts are currently under way, ranging from school choice and new financing schemes to curricular changes and alterations in school governance. I suggested he choose his favorite experiment, invest a chunk of money in it over an extended period, and build in evaluation and research. He said this is what he had been doing, but it was too little and taking too long. He was tired of waiting. At bottom, he suspected that I was just another foot-dragging educator. We have a real challenge ahead of us, convincing our publics that the schools really are trying to do a better job of producing the graduates we all want. Our efforts must be tangible.

Fourth, schools need resources. I don't believe in simply throwing money at problems — we've learned it doesn't work. However, at this moment 37 states are cutting their education budgets. We cannot renew our schools without resources.

Throwing rhetoric at a problem is even less effective than throwing money. Aid targeted at school reform is essential for the years ahead.

Fifth, we need to recognize that the schools cannot remedy all of America's social ills. Since the days of the War on Poverty in the mid-1960s, there has been a tendency to ask schools to take on a growing share of the nation's social problems and later to blame them when the problems persist. Schools are indeed powerful institutions, but they cannot single-handedly overcome inequities in housing and income distribution; compensate for the decline of the family and the church; eliminate the scourge of drugs, teen pregnancy, and neighborhood violence; reinvigorate America's economy; or reestablish the old world order. We must not ask them to do what they cannot do. We must not allow them to become political battlegrounds for competing ideologies and special interest groups attempting to shape the nation's values.

What we must demand of the schools is that they produce more and better-prepared graduates. In his autobiography, Henry Adams wrote of his education at Harvard in the nineteenth century. He said he was forced to study a curriculum conceived in the eighteenth century to prepare him to live in a world hurtling toward the twentieth century. In essence, he lamented an education two centuries behind the times. This, it seems to me, is the challenge and the opportunity facing America's schools. Only if the nation's schools meet the challenge will we have the graduates we all want.

WHAT DO WE WANT
OUR GRADUATES TO BE LIKE?

2

William J. Bennett

I would like to take up the question, "What do we want our graduates to be like?" by offering some general thoughts on education, by posing an "ideal" type of graduate, and by raising some considerations that the current condition of some of our students imposes upon us. I then want to see if we can give an answer that works in the real world for "not simply the best, but the rest."

First, however, some general comments on education. My view is that education's fundamental purpose concerns the nurture and development of intellectual and moral character. It seems to me that that is the central purpose of the enterprise. When the American people are asked what they want from their schools, they consistently put two tasks at the top of their list: First, teach children how to speak, write, read, think, and count correctly; and second, help them to develop reliable standards of right and wrong that will guide them through life.

These views have deep roots in the United States. At the time of our nation's founding, Thomas Jefferson listed the requirements for a sound education in the Report of the Commissioners for the University of Virginia. In this landmark statement on American education, Jefferson wrote of the importance of calculation and writing, and of reading, history, and geography. But he also emphasized the need "to instruct the mass of our citizens in these, their rights, interests, and duties, as men and citizens." Jefferson believed education should aim at the improvement of both "morals" and "faculties."

It's interesting to note, I think, that when I was chairman of the National Endowment for the Humanities, we did a survey of hundreds of influential Americans — Democrats and Republicans; whites, blacks, Asians, and Hispanics; young and old — and asked them to list the 10 books they thought that *every* high school graduate should have read (or at least be familiar with) by the time he or she graduates. There was a general consensus among the books recommended. The syndicated columnist George Will then wrote a column in which he asked his readers to respond to the same question. Their responses were consistent with the original ones we received; in particular, there was a *remarkable* degree of consensus about the first four. They were the Bible, selected plays of Shakespeare, the founding and guiding documents of American political life (such as the Declaration of Independence, the Constitution, the Federalist papers, the Emancipation Proclamation) and the American novel *The Adventures of Huckleberry Finn*. That's a pretty good curriculum for high school juniors or seniors (or, for that matter, a year-long college introductory course in the humanities).

I'll now move on to the topic assigned to me. Clearly, we would like all our graduates to be "ideal," and by that I mean (among other things) someone who can read, write, count, and think reasonably well; who has reliable standards of right and wrong; who possesses a steadiness of purpose; who is smart and ambitious (but ambitious for large and noble ends, not merely self-interested ends); who is tolerant of others; and who is honest, friendly, helpful, and civic-minded. We would like all of our students to demonstrate some of the character traits and success that we find in, say, Colin Powell, or George Bush, or Billy Graham, or Margaret Thatcher. Again, that is something we would like to get, and sometimes we do get it. But we need to face some practical questions, such as: What can we *realistically* hope for from most of our students? Are we prepared to settle for something less than the "ideal" graduate? And what do we want average or below-average students to be like?

Let's take the problem at its hardest point. Let's think about students who are still under the supervision of adults and who are not realistically going to become leaders of nations or outstanding community leaders or world-class doctors or lawyers or scientists; in short, students who are not going to be considered the "Most Likely to Succeed," or even likely to succeed at all. It seems to me that what we want these graduates to be like is similar in type (if not in degree) to what we expect from our "ideal" high school graduate. Let me elaborate.

We want all our high school graduates to be able to read (even if they have to read slowly, maybe while moving their lips or using a finger to follow the words) and to have the ability to decode simple texts. We want all high school graduates to be able to do such things as sign their names, write thank-you notes, and fill out forms. We want them to be able to count pocket change and to balance checkbooks. We also want our graduates to have the ability to speak reasonably well, express ideas, give voice to their beliefs and convictions, articulate feelings at important moments with friends or family members, and express their sense of satisfaction or outrage about events in the public arena.

I also think we should expect our graduates to have some understanding of what it means to work, to learn how to persevere in a task; to be able to start something, finish it, and then to take some justifiable pride in it. It doesn't have to be something on the order of the Sistine chapel; it can be something simple, done in shop or poetry class. But students need to know what work is and why they should take pride in a job — even a simple job — well done.

High school graduates should develop good habits. ("It makes no small difference," Aristotle wrote, "whether we form habits of one kind or of another from our very youth; it makes a very great difference, or rather *all* the difference.") Some good habits we should impart to our students include honesty, persistence in the face of adversity, faithfulness to family and friends, loyalty to country, good manners (if not always having good feelings) toward others, and self-discipline. When I was secretary of education, employers told me over and over again: "Give me an honest person who has the self-discipline to get up in the morning, get to work on time, and works hard, and I'll find a job for that person."

Our graduates should also develop respect of certain sorts: respect for the rights of others, for diversity, for different opinions, for the law, for our most important social institutions, and for the practices of a free society. We don't want our graduates smashing printing presses or using drugs or doing the kinds of things that will cause harm and get them and others in trouble. This is all a part of what it means to be a citizen in a free republic.

High school graduates also need to develop a respect for evidence and learn to draw conclusions based on where the evidence and the facts lead. They need to be able to give valid reasons for much of what they think and believe and do.

Let me suggest the importance of developing a certain kind of attitude, an outlook, a temper of the will. It has to do with a certain *positive* attitude toward life, a geniality of person, a can-do spirit, a willingness to go forward in life, a willingness to say yes if at all possible to worthy ideas, projects, proposals, and endeavors. With this kind of attitude comes the absence of basic resentment (what the kids call a "head case"). We don't want our graduates to feel so embittered that they do not embrace life and its opportunities. I think this attitude is perhaps as important as any other. Yes, we want our students to be careful, to be critical thinkers, and to be law-abiding. But we also want them to like life, and to go after it with vigor and good cheer.

Finally, let me propose five things — five "learned truths," if you will — that everyone should know (or at least think about) before they leave school, for their sakes and for the sake of others.

1. All human beings have worth, but not all human beings have equal merit.
2. Might does not make right.
3. It is true that all people have both an equal right to their ideas and an equal right to express them. But it is not true that all ideas are equal, or should even be treated equally.
4. Just because something feels good doesn't mean one should do it.
5. Despite the canard to the contrary ("You can be whatever you want to be"), most people cannot be anything they want to be. High aspirations should absolutely be encouraged among students, but they should be encouraged realistically.

Let me briefly discuss some of the reactions these truths often elicit from professional educators.

First, let's dispense with one notion that seems to irritate people, but really shouldn't. When educators hear me say that most people cannot be anything they want to be, many construe that as a recommendation of low aspirations for students. That's absurd. The problem with all too many of our students isn't a lack of high expectations, it is that they have high expectations, but they haven't been equipped with the means, the proper tools, to achieve them. And that sets them up for a very hard fall later in life. We're not getting across often enough the point that in order to be an astronaut, or a great artist, or a great performer, students need to learn, to work, to practice, and to engage in the necessary intermediate steps that will take them to their goals and the fulfillment of their aspirations.

I remember once talking to a young woman in high school in New Jersey who told me she wanted to be a pediatrician. I asked her if she was taking chemistry and biology. She said, "No, I'm not, but I'm working with children and have a great deal of affection and devotion to them." Affection for and devotion to children are fine, but if this young lady wants to be a doctor, she's going to have to take chemistry and biology in high school. That's the common sense point I'm making.

Related to this is the notion that unless all our students aspire to become doctors, lawyers, CEOs of multinational corporations, or president of the World Bank, then we have somehow failed them, or they have somehow failed themselves. Students need to recognize that there is no indignity — indeed, that there can be great dignity — in being a teacher, or nurse, or secretary, or plumber, or carpenter, or chef, provided the person wants to pursue such a career, provided the ambition is commensurate with the person's ability and talent, and provided the person is willing to strive for excellence and is ready to be as good as he or she can be in one of those jobs.

Television and the movies argue at least indirectly that the only life worth living is life "in the fast lane." We need to teach our young people a different lesson. Students need to learn, through the example of the adults around them, through what they read, and through what we teach them, that the good life doesn't necessarily entail a "prestigious" job, lots of money, fame, or the responsibility of directing hundreds of people. A good life can be made in many other ways; in fact, it usually is.

Many educators object to the points I've raised, arguing, as I am, that we should proceed with education today much as we proceeded with education 25 years ago. Much is made in contemporary education literature about how much the world has changed, how we are in the midst of a period of rapid social change, and how we are moving toward a future the shape of which is largely unknown. This rapid pace of events is used as an argument for throwing out the old, time-honored practices and replacing them with more "progressive" and novel approaches. It is what C. S. Lewis called "the horror of the same old thing."

Of course, if we closely examine this proposition, we will see that it will fall of its own weight. For one thing, it leads us basically to throw up our hands in despair, since the conclusion is that we do not have any reliable idea of what we should do, or any sense of the means by which to get there. In fact, many of the time-honored practices that have worked in the past — homework, memorization, and drills — *will* work in the future. And the whole notion that the world in all its ways will be so fundamentally different as to be unrecognizable is just plain wrong. We do not know *some* of what the world will be in the future, but we do know much of what the world will be. We know a lot about how people will act, and we know a great deal about the challenges our children will face. We know, for example, that human nature will remain essentially unchanged. All of this despite advancements in technology, science, medicine, and many other fields.

We know, too, that our students will still need to hold jobs, and that they will live in a country with the same basic political institutions (with judicial, legislative, and executive branches), a free press, businesses, schools, and colleges. And we know that most will raise children, live in neighborhoods, and have an array of civic and social responsibilities to meet. There are certain constraints in life, and there are certain constraints in education. If we take the long view of history, we see that the changes that are most relevant to education are changes in form, in appearance, in contingency — *not* changes in the essential realities.

Furthermore, we can say with some confidence that our students will be better off in the future if they are smart rather than stupid, if they are learned rather than ignorant, and if they are skilled and ready rather than unskilled and unready. It is precisely over this issue that a great pedagogical divide takes place. Study after study has shown that the students who are best prepared for life — in terms of getting a college education and a job — are students who have the best grounding in the basic disciplines of English, math, history, and science. Of course, these disciplines have changed somewhat over the years, and the ways we teach them have changed somewhat. That's fine and good. But there is no evidence that a changing world means we should stop teaching students the basic disciplines. In fact, a strong case can be made that the more the world changes, the more important it is for students to have a grounding in things that are enduring and true, knowledge that will serve them in the future. Given the choice between speculating about a whole array of different futures (all of which are by postulation unknowable) or grounding students in the basic disciplines that will help them to develop good habits of mind and heart, I would certainly take the latter. In terms of the curriculum, the best way to proceed is to give our students the best we have in the areas of English, math, history, and science.

We also need to agree once again on the actual purpose of our schools, because if we do not agree on *that*, we are not likely to agree on the means that education should use to serve that purpose. I have often heard at educational conferences that the purposes of the schools are (a) to prepare students for "the radically changed twenty-first century," (b) to help students "be members of an increasingly interdependent world," and (c) to raise students' "social consciousness so they can get on with the task of changing society and the world at large." But in fact none of these is the central purpose of the schools. As I mentioned earlier, the purposes of our schools are (as the American people have it) to nurture and develop moral and intellectual character; to help students speak, read, write, count, and think correctly; and to prepare students to lead productive lives. The American public school is owned by the American public, and the public has a right to its view. Further, I believe this view is the correct one — the one that will best serve students and our nation. Few things do a greater disservice to our students than a trendy, utopian notion of public education that (although much in fashion among certain social thinkers and futurists) has no basis in reality.

Then there is the charge that the kind of curriculum I have proposed might be fine and good for white middle-class students, but it doesn't work for low-income minority students. This is an outrageous, insidious claim; it suggests that what is good for the middle class is not good for the underclass, or what is good for white students isn't good for black or brown students. The damage that this notion has done to minority and underclass students is enormous. It has led to separatist curricula, and watered-down courses for minority students, and given widespread currency to the belief that we should have radically different educations for students according to ethnicity and socioeconomic background.

This leads to what I have called "back-of-the-bus mathematics" and "Jim Crow science." *All* of our students are entitled to the best we have to offer. It is not fair to give white middle-class students the "basic" curriculum and then to shunt other students into narrow disciplinary tributaries based on specious notions of social membership. The purpose of the schools is to make all of our children as smart as they can be, and to make them smart in the same ways. Of course we should recognize that differences in individuality and creativity should be nurtured through different pedagogies, but we need to practice those pedagogies through a common curriculum and a common set of expectations for all our children.

One of the National Educator Award winners, Jaime Escalante, has proved that a challenging curriculum and high expectations are not only a wise course of action, but an achievable one. He has demonstrated at Garfield High School that low-income Hispanic students can excel at calculus — something many people regarded as impossible.

Jaime Escalante told me that some of the greatest challenges to his efforts came from his fellow teachers and counselors who told him that because his students were poor and Hispanic, they would not be able to do calculus. (Some even questioned whether they *should* do calculus. One teacher told Escalante that teaching his students calculus would be "dangerous" because they could never learn it, and the failure would hurt their "self-esteem." Escalante, a Bolivian immigrant, told the teacher, "I have not been in this country very long, but I do know this. For a 16-year-old, low-income Hispanic kid growing up in East Los Angeles, there are a lot of things that are dangerous. Calculus is not one of them.")

Escalante, mindful of the difficult future many of his students would face, gave them the best he had to offer. The results have been clear, and very impressive.

Last year, more than 150 Garfield students took advanced placement in calculus, and many were then admitted to the best universities in the United States. The kind of lives they will have are now within their power to decide. Escalante has helped them to be (as the phrase goes) the best that they can be.

Let's now proceed to the heart of the matter: how we make sure students receive the education they deserve, and how we improve the overall condition of American education. Whether students succeed academically depends in large part on what they study — on the curricula schools offer them. It should come as no surprise that a serious deterioration in the rigor of American elementary and secondary curricula accompanied the precipitous declines in American student achievement.

A Nation at Risk, the landmark 1983 report by the National Commission for Excellence in Education, had especially harsh words for high school curricula, which over the years had become "homogenized, diluted, and diffused to the point that they no longer have a central purpose" (p. 18). The report concluded that "we have a cafeteria-style curriculum in which the appetizers and desserts can easily be mistaken for the main courses" (p. 18). Its authors were distressed to find that 25 percent of credits earned by "general track" students were in "physical and health education, work experience outside the school, remedial English and mathematics, and personal service and development courses, such as training for adulthood and marriage" (p. 19).

To replace this smorgasbord of incoherent class work, *A Nation at Risk* proposed a reinvigorated core curriculum for American secondary schools, one organized around a set of "new basics": four years of English; three years each of mathematics, science, and social studies; one-half year of computer science; and, for those students planning to attend college, two years of a foreign language.

Today, eight years after these recommendations were issued, we are still a long way from providing every American student with a solid academic curriculum. But there are now grounds for hope, and if visible improvements at the high school level are complemented by similar changes in the earlier grades — and are given a full chance to work — we may begin to see substantial benefits in learning.

The Department of Education recently undertook a national study comparing the transcripts of 15,000 1987 high school graduates with those of a comparable group of 1982 graduates. The findings are modestly encouraging. Less than 2 percent of the 1982 sample had completed the academic program suggested in *A Nation at Risk*; in 1987, 12.7 percent of graduating students had done so. When foreign language and computer science classes are omitted from the tally, improvement is more dramatic — from 12.4 percent of 1982 graduates to nearly 30 percent in the 1987 sample.

These figures mark a welcome break from a trend much lamented in *A Nation at Risk*: a 15-year migration of American high school students from solid academic work into vague "general track" courses. The proportion of students in the "general track" dropped from 35 percent in 1982 to 17 percent in 1987. Nearly all of this change reflects movement back into a more rigorous academic curriculum.

Moreover, the distribution of classes appears more focused on basics than it did in 1982. The Department of Education's transcript study shows that 86 percent of 1987 graduates completed a U.S. history course. Only 76 percent of 1982 graduates had done so. And 71 percent of 1987 graduates took at least one semester of civics or American politics, up from 57 percent in 1982.

Students today also take an average of one semester more of mathematics than did students in 1982, and enrollments in advanced math classes (geometry, second-year algebra, trigonometry, and calculus) are all up by at least a third. The number of students in precalculus has more than doubled. Enrollment in remedial or below-grade math is down by a third since 1982. Science shows similar improvement. Only 75 percent of all 1982 graduates had taken a class in general biology; 90 percent of 1987 graduates had done so. The number of students taking chemistry is up by half.

In another sign of improvement, the proportion of American high school graduates who have taken advanced placement (AP) exams has more than doubled, from 4.7 percent to 9.7 percent. A few states have registered startling gains in AP participation. South Carolina's rate has more than tripled to 17.3 percent, and Utah now has more than a quarter of its high school graduates taking AP exams. Nationwide, more schools had candidates sit for AP exams than ever before: 7,776 schools for the 1986-87 school year, compared with 5,827 in 1982-83.

Yet we still have much room for improvement; curricular foolishness has not been eliminated from American high schools, and not all students have shared equally in the national trend toward stronger curricula. Compared with public high schools, private and parochial schools still do a somewhat better job of ensuring that their students take the "new basics" recommended in *A Nation at Risk*. At the same task, suburban schools do a better job than either rural or urban schools. More Asian students (26 percent) take all the "new basics" than do either whites (13 percent) or blacks (9 percent), though racial differences in course taking have narrowed since 1982. Most discouragingly, students remaining in the vocational track are still taking far too few courses in the core disciplines. Among 1987 graduates, only 20 percent of students in vocational education programs took a geometry course, as against 80 percent of their academic track peers. Only 4 percent of them took a science sequence that included both biology and chemistry, compared with 66 percent of students in an academic program.

Although the high school curriculum is stronger today than it was five years ago, the figures just cited suggest the need for still greater improvement. Students are spending more time in solid academic courses of study, but we are not yet seeing a corresponding improvement in their knowledge and skills, which, after all, is the bottom line. This suggests that as improvement in our schools continues, we need to pay more sustained attention to the content of courses in addition to the number and types of courses scheduled. Time on task is not a meaningful yardstick of achievement if our students are not being given a challenging, rich curriculum.

Strengthening the curriculum is one of the single most important things we can do to get our students where they should be — to get the kind of graduates we want.

A second step we need to take is to ensure equal educational opportunity, and the best way to do that is to give parents full choice in the schools (public, private, and religious) their children attend. This will have the effect of introducing competition into education, making education more accountable, fairer, and more equitable. As it stands now, middle-class and affluent parents of students have far more opportunities to send their children to good schools than do poor parents. If upper-middle-class parents do not like the public schools in their neighborhoods, they can pay the money to send their children to private schools. The poor do not have this option, and it is long past time that we should give it to them.

The third thing we need to do is establish an ethos of achievement. I salute programs, such as the Milken Family Foundation National Educator Award Program, that recognize achievement in individual excellence in concrete, specific, and explicit ways. They provide a tremendous opportunity for recognition, and more foundations should be doing this kind of work.

Fourth, we should adopt the idea of school-based management, giving principals more say in the hiring of teachers and holding them accountable for results. As it stands now in American education, very few consequences follow from the results of individual school programs. If a school does well, its principals and teachers are not likely to be rewarded; if a school does poorly, there is no penalty. *Today there are greater, more certain, and more immediate penalties in this country for serving up a single rotten hamburger in a restaurant than for repeatedly furnishing a thousand schoolchildren with a rotten education.* This must change. There need to be consequences for performance in education, just as there are in the business world.

Let me conclude by simply reiterating what I said earlier. The questions in front of us are difficult questions. It is critical at this stage, then, that we first find agreement on what the central purposes of the schools are. If there is no consensus on this first question, this fundamental question, then it's time we have a full-scale debate. Let's recognize, too, that in that debate the people who have the final right to decide are the people who own the American schools, the American public.

Assuming we can agree on clear purposes, let us go back to the business of serving our children, who are, after all, the focus of the enterprise. Let us do so by strengthening the curriculum, by providing the opportunity for every student — regardless of race or socioeconomic status — to have a shot at the curriculum, and by holding our schools accountable. Let us follow the example of the Milken Family Foundation in recognizing excellence. And while we're at it, let us remember to pay tribute and honor to the splendid teachers across this country who have done so much for our children.

With the terms of the debate established by Drs. Levine and Bennett, the National Educator Award recipients gathered for an informal question-and-answer period with the keynote speakers. The session was moderated by Dr. Lewis C. Solmon, then dean of the Graduate School of Education at the University of California at Los Angeles.

RECIPIENT: I would like your views on deconstructionism. According to evidence provided by the case of Duke University, it seems that there are no old rules, that is, that in the context of humanities course work, whatever might fall under the heading of so-called cultural literacy needs to be redefined. How does this development align with the four goals for high school graduates described by Dr. Levine and the single goal suggested by Dr. Bennett?

DR. LEVINE: An article I recently read said that deconstruction is giving manure a bad name. I think there is some truth to that. Regarding deconstructionism as a philosophy, I think it is interesting. There has been a fair amount written on the subject, and it is one that is being heatedly debated. I don't think that it has a central place in the educational system of today, but it is fun to talk about.

DR. BENNETT: I agree. I think deconstructionism is largely a fraudulent academic enterprise. It's something that people can practice at universities because universities provide people great opportunities to be idle. At the elementary and secondary school level, however, you couldn't get away with it. Why? Because the taxpayers would be all over you. Deconstructionism is nonsense, and because it's at Duke, it's nonsense on stilts, but it's still nonsense.

RECIPIENT: There also seem to be no rules, as we've seen recently at Stanford, with respect to assigning the so-called great books.

DR. BENNETT: At Stanford, they go further than dealing with texts. They say in fact that the rules don't apply anymore. In their deconstructionist English department, however, there is still the rule that the chairman make as much money as he can, that he try to get as much money as he can for the people he brings in, that the teaching load be kept as light as possible, and that as few students be seen as possible. Those old university rules have not changed for them.

What I'm saying is that the situation is hypocritical. If *you* went into your classroom and taught Marvel comics — which is what they do at Duke for $23,000 a year in some courses — you would probably hear from your supervisor or principal, and with reason. Frankly, I thought this situation would collapse under its own weight, but it hasn't yet. Intellectually, I think it is indefensible. John Searle, a professor of philosophy at UC Berkeley, has just done an absolutely brilliant critique and refutation of the whole deconstructionist premise.

RECIPIENT: Do you feel that the school should take over the responsibilities of the family and thereby encourage governmental control of individual rights?

DR. LEVINE: No.

DR. BENNETT: I agree, However, I am sure there are many in this room who recognize that they cannot deal only with the students they choose. Great teachers and principals do what they can with the kids they *have*. There are probably a lot of people present who have become de facto (surrogate) parents. I understand that, and I'm sympathetic to it. I also applaud it. But it would be better if parents acted like parents. Not all teachers are parents, but all parents *are* teachers. If, however, parents do not teach their children, it's critical that someone guide those children as best they can. This is the unsung and often the unremunerated task of teachers and administrators, for which we all owe them a lot of gratitude.

DR. LEVINE: My one fear in this area is that over the years we have increasingly asked the schools to take responsibility for the social agenda. With each problem we have been able to locate in a social context, we have asked the schools to be the agent to solve it, and when the schools have been unable to, we've gotten angry with them and said, "Gee, you're just not doing the job we expect."

I think the reality has many aspects: One, schools are not going to be able to overcome the decline of the family. They are not going to be able to overcome the drug problem. Nor teen pregnancy. Nor the renewal of the industrial base of the United States. And they are not going to be able to make the United States newly competitive around the world. They *can contribute* to each one of these issues. The mistake we make is in asking schools to do what they cannot do. I think the need in the next few years is to demand that schools do what they *can* do effectively.

RECIPIENT: Those of us who are early childhood educators are delighted that both Dr. Levine's comments and some of the retreat readings recognize the value of early intervention in preventing many of the problems that emerge in older students. What role is there for the government in the area of early intervention, and what roles for public schools and for the private sector?

DR. LEVINE: A few weeks ago I led a forum on the general topic of what we can do to help our children. The participants included a congressman, the superintendent of schools, the mayor, some judicial activists, education activists, and corporate types, and everyone was wringing their hands and saying, "It's just terrible that we have this problem, and that we're losing our young people."

What concerned me most was that everyone acknowledged the problem, but no one had any idea how to solve it. If I could have one wish granted, it would be to have *Congress* approve an early childhood intervention program. All the other agents have important parts to play. Up in Boston, for example, we've been seeing some fascinating developments between Boston University (BU) and the town of Chelsea. BU has essentially accepted the role of mentor or operator of the Chelsea schools, and one of the first things they have done is build programs that provide health-oriented education for preschool children as well as postnatal care for the youngest children.

I think schools do have a part to play in this regard. I also think corporations have a very large role. Corporations have suddenly been adopting schools, and one of my fears about this kind of relationship is that it exists only in the short term; that corporations will lose interest and pick up another charity. I would love to see corporations make a *serious* commitment to this area.

RECIPIENT: Does Dr. Bennett feel that it is politically possible to give our youngest children what they need to get them off to the best possible start when even programs with demonstrably long-lasting benefits, such as Head Start are underfunded and are not adequately serving the population in need?

DR. BENNETT: Yes. I think it is politically possible, but I think the possibilities would apply to a wider array of programs if they satisfy two criteria: One, that they have a proven record of effectiveness, and two, that they involve the family at as deep a level as possible. I think the more effective we can show legislation to be in strengthening the family, the better the chance of the survival of the programs that are funded.

We need to recognize that from the Great Society forward — that is, in the last 25 or so years — with all the hundreds of billions of dollars that have been spent, some things have improved and some things have gotten worse. A lot worse. And I think that if people are willing to subject their programs to rigorous analysis regarding effectiveness, they will have a stronger claim to the public purse. I also think that kind of analysis is appropriate and should be applied to education throughout the profession.

I'd like to comment on what Dr. Levine said. I agree that society's expectations of schools should be less grand and have fewer facets. We shouldn't ask the schools to do too many things. But that's a different issue from what a student's expectations of his or her teacher or principal are. You say to the school or to society, "Here's what we do, and we don't do anything else," but if you turn out to be a pivotal person in a child's life — as teachers and principals tend to do — it's pretty difficult to turn children down when they come to you for advice or help, whether it be a school-related matter or not.

RECIPIENT: How can the sort of dialogue that we participate in here at the retreat be translated into real proposals? That is, how can our ideas be implemented?

DR. LEVINE: You are an extraordinary group of people. Judging by any standard, you are the best the nation has to offer. I've been talking to many of you about what accounted for your being chosen, and you have indeed done amazing things. You've created programs. You've put new ideas into practice. I think the primary task now is taking the ideas you have been exchanging here at the retreat back to your schools and encouraging your colleagues to think about these kinds of issues. There are many ways that schools can do the sorts of things we've been starting to do here, as we consider who our graduates are and how we want to educate them. There aren't many schools in the country that don't provide opportunities for teachers to get together to plan for the future. It's a question of how to use those plans effectively; of how to make the best use of the summer, for example; of how to bring people together from schools and colleges so we can all talk about the same agenda. I don't think it would take a great deal to bring this about. In a very real way, each school has the ability to make the kind of agenda we're talking about real for its faculty, for its administration, its students.

DR. BENNETT: I don't have anything to add to that. I think Dr. Levine has answered the question very well.

RECIPIENT: Dr. Bennett, what is your perception of the future of multicultural education? How should it be presented in schools, and might you consider expanding your required reading list beyond the four texts you mentioned in your prepared remarks to include readings that depict the lives and histories of the various cultural groupings in America today?

DR. BENNETT: Sure. I have no objection to adding to the list, but I do think it is a good list to begin with. The people in the Bible, by the way, are not exactly Detroit suburbanites. They are not the white middle class. The Bible tells a pretty multicultural story, and it is also rich in stories about women as well as men.

Huckleberry Finn is multicultural in that sense as well. It deals with the essential and underlying problem in American society: slavery.

To repeat, I have no objection to adding books to the list, but let me say — and I know there are those who disagree with this — that I believe that our first responsibility to our students is to introduce them to a common culture of beliefs and principles. What Abraham Lincoln said is true: "We are united not by skin color but by adherence to certain principles of equality and liberty." That is our common heritage. That is what makes us Americans. The responsibility is to carry that heritage forth so that all may be shareholders in it.

I have yet to understand why, in my own case as a child growing up in Brooklyn with four grandparents who each came from a different country — I should have had Hungarian studies, English studies, Irish studies, and German studies. What I *was* entitled to was the best education that this country had to offer.

When I asked my grandparents if we were going to Hungary, my grandfather said, "If we had wanted you to see Hungary, we wouldn't have left. We came to America because this is the land of opportunity and this is the culture that you will learn."

Again, I don't have any objection to expanding the list, but I want children to succeed. I want them to be comfortable in American society. Research is pretty clear about the successful Asian-American students in American schools whose parents tend to regard American education as the most golden of opportunities, and they are right. It is the most golden of opportunities.

Expand the canon, bring in other books, bring in other ideas and notions — but unless we make each of our children, whatever their color or background, shareholders in this common culture that is America, we have not done our job.

RECIPIENT: Dr. Bennett, I have two separate points to make. With all due respect, I imagine all four of your grandparents came to this country by choice, and that makes a big difference. Second, why should all children learn the basics by looking at other people's cultures when they can also learn the basics by looking at their own?

DR. BENNETT: Why do you assume that their own culture is not American? They are Americans, and this culture is neither black nor white. It is American, and it has a lot of pieces to it. Let's meet this issue head on. Should we gloss over slavery? Absolutely not. Should we tell our children about Martin Luther King? Absolutely. Should we talk about the discussion between Injun Jim and Huckleberry Finn on the raft? Absolutely. These are all facts and realities we must address, but because a child coming into a classroom is black, I don't see any reason to assume that that child has an interest in the history of whatever country his great grandfather came from. If that history is something the child wants to study, fine. But I don't see that — in this melting pot — the high school has the responsibility to offer 45 courses.

RECIPIENT: Dr. Bennett, that statement is one of the basic reasons why urban schools are failing.

DR. BENNETT: I disagree. The research of John Ogbu, a professor of anthropology at UC Berkeley, points to the contrast between many of the successful Asian-American students and many black students, and especially to the fact that black students do not see education as a golden opportunity. They see education as an exercise controlled by an oppressive white power system. That perception changes their attitude and their interest in attending school in order to learn.

When I was a proctor at Harvard College, there were many incoming black students. I had one from Harlem who was premed. He had advanced placement in calculus and physics, and after three weeks on the Harvard campus he wanted to switch his major to social relations. Now, social relations is a gut course at Harvard, but people got to this student and said, "This is the course that all of the brothers are taking." Why does this student have to listen to them?

He asked me to sign his course card, and I refused and said, "You want to be a doctor. Don't be pressured into thinking that you can't be a doctor." But he dropped his major, shifted to social relations, and never became a doctor. I think the pressure on kids — particularly minority kids — to conform to someone's notion of what their ethnic identity ought to be is damaging.

DR. LEVINE: Dr. Bennett and I reach roughly the same conclusion on some issues, but we get there in very different ways. At my institute we are just finishing a study that looks at race relations on the college campus. The study also considers gender and ethnicity, and we have found four things occurring among college students.

First, they tend to define themselves in increasingly narrow ways; that is, they define themselves more in terms of their differences than in terms of their commonalities. Their commonality is a very weak notion to them.

The second thing is that the degree of difference between them is decreasing, but a mitosis of sorts is occurring. On one campus, for example, we found a group of gay students that was divided, first, by gender, then by race, and then by the subject they were majoring in — so that we have lesbian science students of color.

Third, we found that students systematically underestimate the extent to which they are involved with one another. This produces two results. After we went to a dance, for example, we asked majority students, "How many blacks do you think attended the dance last night?" and they would answer 10, when, in fact, we had counted 50.

The fourth thing that concerns me is that students of *all* descriptions — whether they're from a majority or minority, male or female — tend to describe themselves as victims. They see themselves as people who are in some ways excluded and being taken advantage of.

With all this in mind, I think a couple of things are critical: One, I think we need a kind of education that cherishes our differences and at the same time affirms our commonalities. The kind of education Dr. Bennett was describing is very important to me.

But two other things are important to me as well. One is that when we talk to minority students on college campuses, and we ask them what they feel about the education that's available to them, they regularly say, "I feel like a guest. I feel uncomfortable and illegitimate." When we looked for evidence of multiculturalism, we found it takes place outside the classroom. In residence halls, in dining rooms, in the remarks of various speakers. But it is not part of the curriculum.

When it *is* part of the curriculum, we create minority studies programs, and we create diversity requirements. What we really need is to have multicultural issues permeate the curriculum. The study of women, ethnic groups, and new populations ought to be part of history. They ought to be part of the sociology curriculum and biology too. They ought to be part of everything we teach in a university or school.

I would add two more elements. I do not think that the way to impart a global perspective is by watering down what we have historically called Western civilization. But I also think Western civilization in and of itself is inadequate, and we can see the consequences of it. Over the last several years we have have been involved in Libya, we've had a peacekeeping force in Lebanon, we've had skirmishes with Iran and a war with Iraq.

The reality for us is that if we are to live in this world in the next few years, we must understand the other cultures that exist. I believe the Koran is as important a book for us as some of the others that we thought were critically important in Western culture. These books *must* be part of the curriculum. When we think of multiculturalism, it is critical that we think of it both domestically and internationally.

DR. BENNETT: I wish it were true that to understand one's adversary would be to avoid conflict, but I'm afraid that with some countries and certain international movements, the more we understand, the more we see the reason for the conflict. The more we understood what Saddam Hussein was about, for instance, the clearer it became that action was necessary. Hitler's Germany was not exactly an obscure, arcane culture. It just happened to be demonic, and the more we knew about it, the more we had to fight. I wish it were true that international understanding would lead to international peace. The problem is that we are better than most countries at international understanding. They don't care a whit for it.

RECIPIENT: This is an observation on culture rather than a question. Here, in the home of "Valley-speak," one of the things we hear most often is "you know, you know." Kids say this because they lack a common cultural experience, and they are begging us to share something with them — something that they themselves can't express — because they don't have that commonality.

RECIPIENT: With so much emphasis on evaluation and the return to basics, how do you propose teaching the "3 Cs": critical thinking, creativity, and continuous learning?

DR. LEVINE: Well, you know — I can't believe you are not teaching most of these things already in some form or other. I am simply asking that they be made explicit. What I'm really requesting is something people have been calling for for a long time: a higher order of thinking. This goes beyond the basics of reading, writing, and arithmetic. What we're talking about here can be taught in any subject matter.

I am a sociologist by training, and before that my background was in the sciences. What I am hoping for is that no matter what the subject matter, we teach students how to think critically; that in whatever exercises we take them through we have them go beyond the mastery of information and ask them to be critical — to know how to raise the right questions and how to find the answers to those questions. We also need to take the next step regarding the kinds of examinations we give students.

Educational creativity is the ability to get students to ask different kinds of questions; to help them to know what kinds of questions are important; to know how to develop answers that aren't short and descriptive but that show some degree of innovation. We can move students in those directions according to how we teach. Continuous learning is the process of asking students to take ever more responsibility for their education and to act in a more autonomous fashion. None of these exercises is intrinsic to a particular discipline. Each can be conveyed in any subject we teach.

DR. BENNETT: Those are Dr. Levine's 3 Cs, not mine. I still think the best way to learn how to learn is to start by learning *something*.

Every time I went to a meeting as education secretary, there would be experts who were going to change the curriculum because the one they had was so terrible and outmoded. I would look around the room and see all these very successful people who had somehow managed to make it through an extremely backward and repressive curriculum of math, English, history, and science.

RECIPIENT: Dr. Bennett, you spoke of schools that watered down expectations and the curriculum for minority students, and yet the fifth point you offered in your conclusion was that not everyone can be what they want to be. Who makes that judgment? How is it made? And when is it made?

DR. BENNETT: The fifth point I made was that not everyone can be what they want to be, that's correct. That was to introduce a note of realism into people's expectations. But a lot more people can learn math than are currently learning it.

Jaime Escalante proved that at Garfield High School, not far from here in East Los Angeles — the school's 80 percent Hispanic — and his calculus class came in fourth in the country last year in advanced placement scores. I asked Jaime if the students gave him a lot of resistance, and he said, "Some did, but I tell the students where they stand."

Jaime went on to tell the story of how he once started in with a calculus class, and a boy got up to leave, and when Jaime asked where he was going, the boy said to see his girlfriend. "Well, if you aren't going to take calculus, then I suggest you go to woodworking class and learn how to make a shoe-shine kit so that when the Anglo businessmen come through LAX airport you can shine their shoes."

And the student got very angry, which was Jaime's intention, and he said, "I don't want to shine any Anglo's shoes!"

And Jaime says, "Right you are. Sit down and study calculus." And now we have 160 of these kids doing advanced placement work in calculus.

Jaime says the strongest resistance he got was from his colleagues, who didn't believe that the children could learn because of their demographics. *That* is a case of institutionalized low expectations.

I don't want to lower the expectations of students. I want their expectations to be realistic. But what they need is a clear sense of the steps to be taken in order to get where they want to go.

DR. LEVINE: Something I have been studying for the last few years is the case of kids who make it who never should have made it. Their backgrounds would tell you that these kids were destined to fail, but lo and behold, they end up with incredible careers. I worry about making decisions about who does what too early.

DR. BENNETT: Right.

DR. LEVINE: But it is very, very important to realize what is possible and what isn't. The key to helping kids to make it and to go far beyond what they might have ordinarily been capable of doing is to treat them the way the educators here are treating their students.

Biographies of people who have made it are fascinating. If you read the stories of Booker T. Washington and Richard Rodriguez and their very different kinds of views, and you compare them with the biography of Norman Podhoretz, you see different eras and different races, but the stories could have been written by the same person. In the lives of each of these people somebody walked in and said, "You matter. You are very good, and there are enormous possibilities for you." That person then served as a kind of Daniel Boone. He'd say, "I'm going to take you from the culture and the world that you are in to a very different kind of world. I'm going to help you see the map and to get there."

I think enormous things are possible for all kinds of kids, and I think that is the reason that the educators here have been so successful.

RECIPIENT: Why is it that this country is willing and able to commit billions of dollars and hundreds of thousands of people to knock the stuffing out of Saddam Hussein, but it's unwilling to commit a proportional amount of dollars and people to improving our educational system?

DR. BENNETT: I think I should go after Dr. Levine, because once I answer I'll probably want to get out of the room.

DR. LEVINE: I think that's a great question. And I don't understand the situation either.

DR. BENNETT: Okay, I'll answer it. The panel solidarity has just collapsed. We *are* willing to spend billions of dollars. The bill for American education this year is $400 billion. That's a lot of money. We spend more than anybody in the world. I don't think the problem is how much money we spend. It's how we spend it. I don't have any objection to spending more money, provided we get better results and more accountability.

What the Milken Family Foundation has done here is exemplary. Do I think that the people here should be making bigger salaries? Sure I do. But I think a lot of the people in the classroom teaching today shouldn't be making any salary at all. And until those representing the teaching profession are prepared to accept more general standards of accountability, that's not going to change.

I have had this argument with Albert Shanker, president of the American Federation of Teachers, and Mary Futrell, president of the National Education Association, time after time. The educators here are great, but not all educators are, and American taxpayers have seen too many examples of bad teaching and of bad schools for them to say, "Let's raise all their salaries."

If you make it selective, and you say, "Let's do an evaluation, and let's reward our good teachers," I believe that 85 percent of the American people would say, "Fine."

When I was secretary of education, I went to Chicago public schools, and I called them the worst schools in America. There *are* some great schools in Chicago, however. Kevin McCann is here from La Salle Language Academy. I went to La Salle, and it's a terrific school. Do I think Amy Narea, the principal, and Kevin McCann should be making more money than they make? You bet. But as a condition of increasing the expenditure, I want to see the lousy teachers in Chicago schools taken out of the classroom. There was a teacher whose classroom I walked into — as secretary of education, for crying out loud — who said to her class, "I don't know who these people are, but if you don't give me any trouble, I won't give you any. You don't raise a ruckus, I won't give you any homework."

I say, "Fire that teacher! Fire her. Get her out, because she gives the lie to everything we stand for!"

SUPERINTENDENTS' VIEWS: WHAT DO
WE WANT OUR GRADUATES TO BE LIKE?

4

Eve Bither, Henry Marockie,
Eugene Paslov, and
Charles Toguchi

In order to provide as complete a basis as possible for the afternoon workshop discussions, four of the participating state superintendents of education presented counterpoints to Drs. Levine and Bennett. To paraphrase the remarks of Dr. Eugene Paslov of Nevada: State superintendents must provide leadership to find solutions to statewide problems in education; they must take action to support school officials, teachers, students, and local school boards, and in this capacity they make important decisions affecting all the students, teachers, and administrators in a given state. Thus, when restructuring occurs, or special programs for diverse students are implemented, or schools take on such new responsibilities as preschool intervention, frequently state superintendents have supported such initiatives. These presentations were intended to provide the perspective of several states' chief educational policymakers.

DR. EVE BITHER,
MAINE COMMISSIONER OF EDUCATION

The topic of this retreat focuses on outcomes and what all students should know and be able to do by the time they graduate. This subject is actually a very complex process, a process that should be duplicated in each one of our states, at both state and school levels. These are difficult questions that address the very values we as a nation, as a state, and as a community hold.

This is also a process that Maine started more than 18 months ago, when our governor appointed the Maine Commission on a Common Core of Learning. That commission worked for more than 12 months to develop a book of the same name, the content of which is now being debated in many schools throughout our state. Two members of the commission, teacher Joan D'Agostino and principal Jeannette Condon, are among the recipients of this year's National Educator Award.

The process undertaken by the Maine Commission was very difficult, but it was a process that our business community, our schools, our legislative leadership, and many others agree was necessary and valuable. We are now at the stage where important action must be taken on the basis of this document. As a practitioner, I believe I hold a greater sense of urgency than I detected in either of our keynote speakers. I assume that is owing to the fact that, as a practitioner, I have less academic leisure than that enjoyed by our keynote speakers.

Arthur Levine was very interesting and informative on the various cycles of school dissatisfaction, and I was almost seduced into thinking we were able to take the time necessary to reflect and come up with necessary courses of action. Bill Bennett, too, reminded us of many current and effective school practices. Be all that as it may, I have a very different sense of the window of opportunity available to us if we are going to make the profound changes necessary — rather than the incremental changes suggested — for *all* of our children to succeed.

Fine-tuning the current system will not make this success possible. Fine-tuning the system that now exists by incremental changes might be compared to rearranging the deck chairs on the *Titanic*. Something more dramatic is needed.

If we *do* believe that all kids can learn — and learn more — then we must accept the students we now have in their individual totalities and see them as the ones to whom the system must adjust, rather than expect them to adjust to the system we have. This belief includes also recognizing the social conditions of our students and their families, whether those families are nuclear or fragmented, effective or dysfunctional.

I want to remind you, too, of what one of our great heroes, Willie Sutton the bank robber, said when asked, why he robbed banks. His answer: "That's where the money is." When asked, "Why the schools?" I say, "Because that's where the kids are."

I believe very firmly that the government and citizens and parents are all demanding results. And unless we act quickly, we are in danger of losing their support. Therefore, I would like to discuss those actions I think are now necessary in order to bring about what we all want.

First, I think it is essential that — as individuals and as states — we accept a vision of the knowledge, skills, and attitudes we expect from all our students. We need a definition of these expectations, and it should be as detailed and comprehensive as the times demand.

Second, it follows naturally that we must examine the curriculum and instructional practices in our schools in order to bring about that vision. Those practices and curricula need to accommodate a personalized approach allowing for uncommon means of instruction to help students attain common goals. Some of the questions we face include the following:

- How can we be more effective in our practices?
- What should we teach?
- In what sequence should those subjects be taught?

- Is it not time to end the perniciousness of tracking, particularly in our high schools?
- Why is it that we make time a constant in our courses rather than giving the time necessary to reach the outcomes in which we believe?

Third, once we have agreed on common outcomes, we need an assessment system that goes beyond our current paper-and-pencil tests to a more authentic demonstration of what students are able to do. If we believe that being able to write well is important, then it is important that we provide all our students with the opportunity to demonstrate through writing what they can do. If problem-solving skills are a goal, then multiple-choice tests should most likely be abandoned in favor of posing problems to be solved.

Fourth, if profound changes are demanded and expected of our schools, then it is critically important that all of us — teachers, administrators, state departments, the higher education system, school boards, and others — find new ways of working together, of raising questions, of finding the time for reflecting on our practices. I am talking about the continuing need for professional development of the highest quality.

All of us here for the three days of this retreat are very fortunate and very grateful to the Milken Family Foundation for allowing us an opportunity to experience this very high quality of professional development as well as a time for reflection. I would like you to raise your hand if you believe that a regular opportunity such as this one exists for the majority of teachers in your state. I see one ... two ... three hands. I think that is an indication of the need for more opportunities for professionals in our schools to engage in this critical work as part of their regular working day. Wednesday from 3:00 to 5:00 in the afternoon will not do.

While schools cannot solve all the problems of society, or perform the functions of all the social agencies of church and family, schools can and should act as convenors of those individuals and groups whose work is limited and linked to our students' health and welfare. We need to ask for and we need to insist upon that support, perhaps first for those students at greatest risk, on a personal case management basis, and later, hopefully, for all.

My experience as a teacher of physics, as an administrator, and now in my current position, tells me that unrealistic expectations on the parts of our students are usually not the problem. Too often our system has very different expectations and messages for our children. Application to particular colleges is discouraged for some of our students, and there are sometimes limited expectations — and limited aspirations — due to a family's name or socioeconomic status. I would remind you of what Bill Bennett had to say earlier — against low expectations — when he spoke of Jaime Escalante.

All too often for kids, low aspirations are encouraged at home as well as at school. In my own experience in Maine, there was a valedictorian in our northernmost county who had great doubts about applying to the best colleges. Her English teacher encouraged her to apply to Harvard, where she was accepted and where she made the Dean's List in her first semester.

We also had a physics student who, after getting 700 on her college boards, said she wanted to be a dental hygienist. I asked her why, if she liked teeth and pain, she didn't become a dentist. And she did.

I want to conclude by sharing something about my own heroes. When I was 10 years old, I found out about Madame Curie, and I said, "That is what I'm going to be. I'm going to be a chemist and win the Nobel Prize." Instead, I've ended up as a central European immigrant to this country, and I leave it to you to decide. I think there's no doubt that my aspirations were too high.

I conclude with a quote from Winston Churchill, my other hero, who said, "It is not enough to say we tried. We have got to succeed in doing what is necessary." And I congratulate all of you for doing what is necessary.

DR. HENRY MAROCKIE,
WEST VIRGINIA COMMISSIONER OF EDUCATION

I'd like to add a word to Dr. Levine's comments earlier about critical thinking. It comes from one of our teachers, who asked a fifth grader, "What is thinking?" And the response from the child, Cissy, was, "Thinking is like when you're doing math and getting the answers all right." But young Jason's response to Cissy was, "No, you do thinking when you don't know the answer." Now, *that's* critical thinking, Dr. Levine.

With regard to some of our other discussions at the retreat, to the functions of the school, and to the kind of graduates we would like to have, I would like to add some personal observations.

Governor Gaston Caperton and I recently visited a West Virginia school where we met four children who made quite an impression on us. We saw one child, a little girl who was handicapped and confined to a wheelchair, who was in a physical education class that, to its credit, made no distinction between her and the able-bodied children.

We saw a child with no arms and with crippled legs who had been taught by special education teachers to feed himself by placing a fork between his toes. When we encountered him, he was at a lunch table, just bending down, eating his lunch with his classmates.

Then there was the little deaf girl whose school went out into the community and found a volunteer who could sign with the child. That woman now goes everywhere with the child and has become a regular part of the school program.

Finally, we saw a first grader, a little guy, who had had a rather intense confrontation with a pit bull, but whose teacher was compassionate and empathic enough to get the boy right back into the normal rhythm of the class.

Now, that school is certainly dealing with those children and their needs differently from what would have been the case 15 or 20 years ago. And we need that kind of adaptation. Some of today's statistics are frightening. Children today have a one in five chance of becoming illiterate adults. In our institutions — not only schools, but banks, federal agencies, business institutions — it's clear that with the explosion of knowledge and technology, dramatic changes are necessary.

Dr. Levine indicated that he would like to see the federal government embark upon an extensive early childhood intervention program. There's no question that such an initiative on the part of the government would have a crucial impact on the schools.

Dr. Levine also indicated his belief that the schools are not the villains but the victims. He also stated that we should try to do what we do best. On the other hand, Dr. Bennett indicated that his preference is for the teaching of math, science, English, and social studies. When you put these ideas together, they don't accommodate a diverse school population, and they certainly don't allow for the kind of diversity Governor Caperton and I saw at the school we visited.

The fact of the matter is that perception is reality. And whether we like it or not, the school is the best institution, or at least has the best opportunity, for affecting social issues in our country. On what do I base that belief? In West Virginia, as in most other states, more than 70 percent of the budget is earmarked for schools.

The retreat has considered the issue of reform from many perspectives, but we have not focused sharply on the importance of providing teachers with enough time to be reflective, to be decision makers, to exchange ideas, to plan and to develop as professionals. Wouldn't it be great for you elementary and secondary teachers to have the privilege enjoyed by your higher-education counterparts of teaching 6-12 hours a week and having the balance of the time to plan and reflect? Public schools need that kind of restructuring, and if more time of that sort becomes available to educators I think we can successfully see through the reforms we need.

DR. EUGENE PASLOV,
NEVADA SUPERINTENDENT OF EDUCATION

At the risk of oversimplifying, Dr. Levine tells us that things are different now, that they have always been different, and that they are going to continue to be different, but that schools *can* make a difference. He suggests there is going to be a shift in emphasis from process to outcome, that we need accountability, that schools need time to effect change, and that schools need resources — they need money. He has also observed that schools need to focus on doing what they do best and not try to solve all of society's ills.

Regarding the question of whether the schools dare change the social order, I think Dr. Levine's position gives us a lot of hope. Dr. Bennett, on the other hand, left me with the impression that he believes if we only return to some past "Ozzie and Harriet" notion of the family, and if we adopt a corresponding methodology, that everything will work out very well.

Without revealing any bias, I agreed with everything Dr. Levine had to say and with nothing of Dr. Bennett's remarks. My role, like that of my counterparts, is to provide leadership and to help find solutions to statewide problems in education; to take action; to support school officials, teachers, students, and local board members; and to try to unravel some of the complex problems we face. When I attend conferences such as this retreat, I think as the classroom teacher I used to be, and I look to steal ideas. Who has an idea? Who has something that's going to help us? I thought Arthur Levine had a number of good ideas: higher expectations, a higher order of skills from all students, preschool child care with strong parenting components. These are things we *must* do. There is no Ozzie and Harriet family. There probably never was and never will be. The fact of having children does not provide instant mastery of parenting skills. We desperately need to move into preschool care and child care with parenting components.

Dr. Levine also spoke to multicultural understanding and was quite clear about what is called for. Although such understanding may not preclude future wars, it will at least give us a more compassionate understanding of the global humanity of which we are a part.

Dr. Levine did not give us any easy formulae for solving societal ills, but he left us with some hope, and, personally, I find that very satisfying.

Dr. Bennett, on the other hand, made a number of points with which I strongly disagree. The notion of returning to the nuclear family is one of them. The family, as we all know, has been undergoing dramatic changes, and we have to find more creative ways of dealing with those changes. Teaching kids to read and count is not sufficient. We have to teach them much more than that.

I have some responsibility for textbook selection in Nevada, and Dr. Bennett's reading list would get me in a lot of trouble, I can tell you. The Bible as a textbook would cause me a lot of grief, although I do think it has some value. As for the Constitution, the Bill of Rights and the Federalist papers, they are all wonderful documents, but the textbook publishers have applied "readability formulae" to them and turned these wonderful pieces of literature into unintelligible pap. It's unfortunate, but that is exactly what has happened. If we could give kids the original documents, I would agree with Dr. Bennett.

As for *Huckleberry Finn* as a seminal piece of fiction, there are some critics who would argue that it chronicles the racism of the period and does very little to enhance multicultural understanding. Nevertheless, I can appreciate the fact that among critics of American literature, there may be some debate. But I think there are a lot of works that would need to be included for a multicultural education in American arts and letters.

Public school teachers really do believe that all kids can learn. And they always get a little edgy when the subject is the truncating of kids' dreams. When the distinction between worth and merit is being made, we want to be very careful about who makes that decision for our kids.

Another point: Money does make a difference. Public school teachers know that. And to say that we have enough money to do what needs to be done in American education is, to my way of thinking, wrong.

The issues are complex, but they are soluble. Our speakers have helped us, and I would like to thank them both. What we need now is vision in the schools. We need the right goals and high expectations. We need to emphasize the importance of schooling, and we need to have the freedom of creativity to do what Dr. Bither has suggested, that is, to reconsider altogether our educational delivery system.

MR. CHARLES TOGUCHI,
HAWAII SUPERINTENDENT OF EDUCATION

In my opinion, education is the most critical profession in the world, and though Hawaii is in many ways unique, we have many of the same problems that have been discussed here.

Dr. Levine cited a number of issues that I would agree deserve our close attention: inadequate salaries, lack of resources, the changing ethnic mix among students, and lack of traditional forms of support. I agree with his observation that *all* social institutions are being left behind in times of rapid change — not just schools. He also zeroed in on the fact, with which I heartily concur, that schools cannot "do it" alone. That is why so many of us have developed partnerships over the years.

The issue that most illuminated Dr. Levine's presentation, in my view, was that of preschool intervention. Parenting programs, prenatal and postnatal care — these are going to be among the major factors changing our educational system.

Dr. Levine also made the important point that in education the emphasis must shift from process to outcome. The great need that he described is to achieve a commonality of outcomes with a multiplicity of ways of achieving them. The imperative for this shift explains why many of us are providing more flexibility, such as site-based management, in our schools.

Dr. Levine also noted the schools' need for freedom and accountability; I believe that everyone needs to understand fully the relationship between these two requirements. And he also spoke of the need for time, a need I strongly endorse, especially vis-à-vis educators who can benefit so much from time together to talk and plan.

In closing, I will say that I found Dr. Bennett's presentation very narrow. Though he talked about the kind of graduate we want, he didn't put forth any solutions to our educational problems. And as for his final "recipe" of learned truths that add up to the graduate we want, I disagree. All children are different, and I don't think such a recipe will work for all.

PRACTITIONERS' VIEWS: WHO DO WE WANT OUR GRADUATES TO BE? 5

Katherine Nouri Hughes

Where the keynote talks established complementary premises on which to consider the retreat's theme, the afternoon workshops, organized by discipline and grade level, elaborated those premises with experiences, confirmations, and intuitions. What issued from more than 200 teachers and administrators, from 18 workshops, from every quadrant of the country, and from the full range of disciplinary perspectives was a list of qualities — far-ranging in their detail but strikingly unified in what they constituted: the graduate of these educators' hopes.

The themes behind the terms ranged from definitions of the individual to depictions of twenty-first-century society, with much discussion of the academic endeavor in between. Toward the personal pole were hundreds of observations about character traits, about morals and values, about aspirations and cultural diversity, and about the effects on students of the fractured family. At the other extreme were the imperatives of a rapidly changing, technology-laden global village.

Educators want our high school graduates to be healthy, whole human beings. On this, they are unanimous. They also agree that in today's community, whether local or global, the making of that sort of graduate is complex and often difficult.

What does it mean to be healthy and whole? The importance of self-esteem in children and teenagers is central and was credited by every group of educators. Self-esteem cannot be taught, most agreed. It develops within. A good teacher can elicit self-esteem, can shine the light of approval on it, but he or she can't impart it. The word *education*, it has been pointed out, literally means leading forth what is within. In that sense, then, self-esteem and self-confidence can be educated.

Many components of self-esteem, all salutary, were cited by the educators at the retreat. These include composure, self-sufficiency, self-respect, discipline, and that often misunderstood and maligned trait, pride. These are key qualities in a student if he or she is going to succeed in school — and take pleasure in it — rather than merely survive the experience.

Many of the personal qualities the retreat participants said they want to see in our graduates relate to the increasing ethnic and cultural diversity of the United States. Hence, tolerance, compassion, empathy, and adaptability were qualities repeatedly invoked.

Nor is simply caring about one's neighbor going to suffice. For caring to have meaning, it must be demonstrated. The graduates we want should be activists; they should be courageous and fully engaged participants in their worlds, conscious of, knowledgeable about, and committed to the protection of their environment.

Closely related to the traits of activism are those connected to problem solving. The educators spoke repeatedly of critical thinking, of the ability to relate what is learned in school to what is demanded by life, of perseverance and curiosity, and of the skills required for "coping" in a tumultuous world.

A number of the personal characteristics cherished and cited by the educators were reiterations of the keynoters' references. Enthusiasm, open-mindedness, tolerance (which was yoked to both empathy and respect), and the quality that arguably underpins all the others: hope.

Overlapping and in many instances supporting these traits of personality are the values that the educators hope their graduates will develop and hold. We want good people, all concurred. But what are the values that add up to a person's being "good"? All agreed that it was difficult to agree on a core set of values. Certainly a strong ethical sense is on the list (interestingly, the term *honest* seemed to give way to *ethical*), especially as preparation for the postgraduate experience; a respect for power and, conversely, the understanding that power should not be abused; a broad-gauged "spiritual awareness" (not to be confused with religious affiliation or sensibility); and, comprising many of those values the educators held dear, the understanding that "it is not what one has that matters, it is what one gives." Put differently, it's not what one does that counts, but who one is.

A key method for determining, defining, and expanding who one is can be found in goalsetting. Although all agreed that having aspirations and striving for them are both central to the kind of graduate we want, most workshops agreed that the nature and level of those aspirations should be very carefully considered. It was clear, moreover, that the setting of goals for students by *educators* and the setting of goals for students by *students,* though related, are different enterprises.

William Bennett's keynote injunction that students set their goals well inside the boundaries of realism — and that the onus is on teachers to have them think in those terms — elicited considerable but by no means unanimous opposition. The majority of educators held that students are "empowered through high aspirations" and, following from this, that many teachers would do well to expect more, not less, from their students. "We should make them feel capable" — that "they can be what they want to be," many said. In other words, if educators are going get students to expect that much from themselves, the prior issue is for teachers to expect at least that much from students.

For students to conceive and set their own goals, they need "more information on their options," some said; they need to be in touch with their immediate world. The inspiration of a good biography can often be an important supplement to drier data. Students also need strong models "from the top down"; these should include "everyone from the president of the United States to school principals." Nearly all agreed that what students most need as they learn to discern ends from means is *vision*: an unobstructed view of the possibilities on their horizons and the determination that the right possibility can be reached.

Moving from the individual to the collective realm, the educators roundly agreed that a sense of responsibility is critical. First, of course, is the responsibility the student owes to him- or herself. It is this that engenders the all-important sense of self-esteem and self-respect. Responsibility to self is also strengthened by the ability to evaluate and judge one's own actions. If a student is self-critical, a number of educators agreed, a sense of responsibility will be second nature.

Consciousness of — and conscientiousness toward — one's world is a natural by-product of individual responsibility. Starting with the world closest to home is responsibility to the community, which can take the deeply gratifying form of volunteer work. A sense of responsibility to the country does not go without saying. The educators were explicit about the need for cultivating respect for and a sense of duty to the maintenance of our democratic system of government. A sense of "global stewardship" is equally important for students to have, as the ratio of Earth-space to inhabitants diminishes.

Teachers, principals, and administrators have known for a long time that their duties far exceed the boundaries of education. To a person, they agree that the conditions that put a child "at risk" are rapidly increasing and stretching the work, if not the mandate, of schools past all reasonable limits. What *does* a teacher do when a kindergartner comes to school ill clad and unfed? When a seventh grader is pregnant? When a 15-year-old is addicted to crack or heroin or alcohol? How are educators, whatever their jobs, supposed to redress the imbalance of love in so many children's lives?

The educators offered more confirmations of than solutions for the bleaker truths of the school environment. Kids need to know that the breakdown of the nuclear family has become a fact of life, said one teacher. Children who have become accustomed to neglect and abuse need to know they are not alone in their plight and that there are support groups — accessible through school — that can help them. Students also need to be told — by their teachers — that their classmates are not adversaries, but potential allies. The support of peers can be as potent as any form of assistance for children and teenagers of all ages suffering from neglect and abuse.

More and stronger school partnerships with health and business organizations were also suggested as undergirding for overburdened schools and educators. One teacher described the "Life School" within her school — a program that teaches some of the "coping skills" necessary for some children to contend with the basics of everyday life. Another teacher summed up the real meaning for all too many children of today's worst demands: "We should never forget that for some children, it is nothing less than an act of courage to come to school at all."

Some of the original aims of elementary and secondary education, if altered, nevertheless remain intact. Although there remains considerable dissension on what constitute the so-called basics of education, educators speak with one voice on the need for these hard-to-define tools.

The ability to communicate tops the list of crucial basic skills for high school graduates, and literacy is the fulcrum on which all other communication skills balance. Although literacy may seem the ultimate in basics, it was cited by these educators with a frequency that made it clear that the ability to read and write does not go without saying among high school graduates.

Other key communication abilities cited by the educators ranged from the rudimentary talent of conversing fluently to an understanding of how to develop and defend an argument. On the more sophisticated end of the communication spectrum, the capacities to resolve conflicts, to weigh alternatives, and to separate fact from fiction were also cited.

A number of teachers noted the importance of open communication at home in fostering communications skills in school. In the same vein, one teacher expressed the belief that since students may or may not get this kind of boost from parents and since the one place communication skills can't be taught is on the job, it is particularly incumbent on schools to teach students how to express their thoughts and feelings.

Other skills, qualities, and school benefits termed basic included a love of learning, self-sufficiency, subscription to the work ethic, and a willingness to cooperate.

Basic academic skills needed by our graduates (in addition to the "3 Rs") include history — which encompasses personal heritage — geography, natural science, and a combination of computer and core technological competency. A conversance with current events, the knowledge of how to read a newspaper, and what one teacher termed an "ability to work the system" were cited as additional routes to productive membership in society.

Closely aligned with the subject of basics is the curriculum — the grid on which those basics are presented. A number of teachers stated that the curriculum should have an internal logic and integrity. The subjects a student studies should have meaning not only in and of themselves, but also when taken as a whole. One teacher suggested that information be taught across disciplines and grades and by theme. Take the theme of light, she posited, and have a science teacher, an English teacher, and a math teacher treat it from their different perspectives.

The last basic skill with which our graduates should be endowed, creative expression, brought the realm of the arts to the foreground and in many ways made it a scrim through which the development of graduates' attributes can be seen. Aesthetic sensibilities, critical listening skills, and fertile imaginations are important qualities for our graduates, and they can and should be reinforced through exposure to the arts. "The problem," according to many of the educators, "is selling this concept to the public and having it included in the budget."

Only slightly more than half of all states require an arts program in the basic curriculum — a wasted opportunity, said the educators, because the arts cover such a vast range of experiences that yoke entertainment and education and hitch the pair to the graduate we want. Some educators observed that an appreciation of the arts introduced students to modes of thought and experience they otherwise would miss. Others averred what sounded like the opposite — that the arts provide extra illumination of and additional access to the basics of education. The net effect on students of a rich arts component, however it may be construed, is a marked increase in personal fulfillment and a greater appreciation of individual differences.

Differences, similarities, diversity, commonality — the terms of the keynoters' sharpest debate — did not divide the ranks of educators proportionally. The majority of the educators hewed to the position that ethnic and linguistic diversity are permanent and increasingly important facts of American educational life — features that should be at the very least acknowledged if not, more appropriately, honored.

"We need to research our pre-American history to see how rich and diverse the world is," said one teacher. "We need a global perspective that includes the need for multilingualism," declared another. Whether the proper metaphor is the melting pot or the tapestry, a significant majority of educators agreed that children should be educated in cultural differences, especially those they see played out around them.

The benefits of a grounding in cultural diversity include a basic respect for others, an appreciation for their contributions and a "tolerance for their weaknesses." "We should look for underlying similarities," as one teacher summed up the tolerance of most educators, "while acknowledging the growing desire for maintaining distinct cultures."

PART II

HOW DO WE GET
THE GRADUATES WE WANT?

THE MORAL DEVELOPMENT OF OUR NATION'S CHILDREN: THE ROLE OF THE PUBLIC SCHOOL

6

Nancy Magnusson Fagan

In a recent New York Times commentary, Albert Shanker, president of the American Federation of Teachers, illuminated a largely unexamined conflict between teaching cultural differences and teaching moral values. Making a compelling argument for the importance of multicultural education, he wrote: "If only we understood where other people were coming from, if only we had more sensitivity to their cultures — we might not be so wedded to our own points of view. And we might have a better chance of avoiding the conflicts that come from ethnocentrism" (Shanker, 1991, p. E7).

Shanker also posed the question of the potential conflict between respect for cultural differences and the rendering of moral judgments: "Do we really want our students to respect and accept the values, beliefs and attitude of other people no matter what they are? Is every value, belief and attitude as good as every other?" (p. E7).

Shanker resolved the dilemma by arguing that we must teach our children about the values and customs of others, but also consider the moral worth of those values and customs as well as our own. Is apartheid permissible, for example? Should author Salman Rushdie be condemned to death because he wrote a book that offends the religious beliefs of others? Shanker concluded that "by approving practices which would not be tolerated here or in any other democracy, they [the proponents of value-free education] are saying that some people should be held to lower standards than others, implying a kind of moral superiority that is hardly consistent with multi-cultural and global education" (p. E7).

Since its inception, the American public school has upheld its mandate to prepare the nation's children for participation in a democratic society. It has done this by instilling a respect for law and individual rights as well as by promoting voluntary participation by the common weal and by engendering concern for the common good (Lickona, 1988b).

Historically, the school shared with the family and with religious institutions the responsibility for teaching core values such as honesty, integrity, self-respect, and justice (Hall, 1991). The traditional role of the public school was to reinforce values already instilled by parents and imbued by religion.

Today, schools face the unprecedented challenge of instilling values largely without the participation of the family or organized religion. Traditionally, values and religion have been welded, and values issuing from religion have provided the authoritative basis for decisions concerning right and wrong. The reasons for being good were taught in church or at the synagogue, and the ways to be good were taught at school and at home. When school prayer was banned, teachers feared that any reference to religion or values might be construed as doctrinaire. As a result, many teachers chose to avoid the issue, not only of religion but also of values.

The "values-clarification" curriculum of the 1960s and 1970s stemmed from a widely held desire among educators to continue teaching core values. This curriculum relied on a relativistic approach that replaced the former model of absolute values.

The values-clarification curriculum was a specific response to the societal shifts of those decades, shifts that included new family constellations and new working patterns of parents. As American society was becoming more diverse, both a respect for that diversity and an updated decision-making capacity were imperative.

The 1980s and 1990s present a new challenge: the need for core values in the context of social diversity. Hindering a response to this challenge is the lack of consensus among community members on such issues as the role of schools, the proper upbringing of children, and even a concern as fundamental as the consequences of behavior. This challenge, moreover, has been transferred to the schools. Schools are now expected not only to reflect a community's values, but also to influence and instill them — and all while honoring the social diversity of community constituents.

The values that a community shares are not as obvious as they once were. Values must be specifically identified by the community. They must exist outside the context of religion, though not necessarily apart from nationalism, and they must reflect cultural diversity. Educators are advising schools to enlist the support of the larger community as the schools work to establish core values, since it is believed that the broader the basis of values, the more readily they will be adhered to.

The role of the school in the exercise of determining and instilling values is evolving. Never before have schools been expected to bind communities; if they are to do so now, they must have a penetrating understanding of the values cherished by their communities' various constituents.

Commonly held values of learning communities include nonviolence, respect for oneself and for others, honor, integrity, freedom of instruction, respect for nature, respect for one's elders, belief in the importance of contributing to society, and belief in the sanctity of life and liberty. Thomas Lickona (1988b) refers to commonly held values endorsed by school communities as the fourth and fifth Rs: respect and responsibility.

In order to have an impact on community behavior, core values identified by a school community must be widely disseminated and endorsed. Mission statements formulated by schools and communities are useful means for such dissemination. Teachers and students can be encouraged to integrate into their regular discussions such ideas and terms as *doing good*. Teachers can be urged to keep notions of cooperation, consideration, and respect in the front of students' minds.

Once a set of core values is established in a community, it follows that it will take hold in the school community, and it will do so by means of guidance programs, student government, peer groups, and parent involvement programs. In high school particularly, guidance programs and student government are effective channels for the transmission of values, both to individuals and to the group.

Various service projects not only offer students extracurricular opportunities for reinforcing core values, they also tend to put students in touch with adults who further strengthen these beliefs.

In-service training for teachers is essential to developing strong role models. Through this training, teachers can learn specific techniques of conflict resolution and methods that will help them pass core values along to students, an exercise the success of which is very much a function of a teacher's creativity and energy.

It is generally agreed that values are most effectively absorbed by students when they are taught both in the context of regular academic subjects, such as social studies and literature, and on their own. Certain curriculum units lend themselves well to the teaching of values and skills that can enhance self-esteem, such as decision making skills, respect for others, and the general consequences of behavior such as drug abuse.

Some instruction methods may be more conducive to the imparting of values than others. Cooperative learning, for example, may be more effective in engendering respect for others than tracking might be. Similarly, recognition programs, such as "Catch a Kid Being Good," can provide strong reinforcement, as can special class activities, such as nature trips and even programs in martial arts. A creative teacher who is conversant with the community's values will find endless opportunities for instilling those values in his or her students.

The participation of parents in this endeavor is crucial, and the onus is on the school to find ways of involving them. Suggested methods range from offering free meals and baby-sitting to visiting the parents in the home. When schools encounter resistance from parents who feel they are being "indoctrinated," often they can strengthen the appeal by tying the values to the community or even to the nation.

Though some teachers are bold enough to teach values in isolation, most prefer to seek the ratification of community and parents. Individual teachers make a difference in the classroom; school communities supported by parents make a difference in a democratic society.

Allen A. Mori

The failure of the American public school to provide an equal educational opportunity for all children has reached crisis proportions. Fortunately, the public is conscious of the crisis, and numerous governors and state legislatures continue to press their efforts to make American education responsive to the needs and talents of this country's increasingly diverse student population.

Consider the case of California. Recent state census data and estimates provided by educational demographers such as Hodgkinson (1986a) indicate a decline in the birthrate among Caucasians to 1.7 children per female, while the birthrate for Hispanics is 2.8 children per female. Immigration patterns also affect the changing ethnic composition of California schools. More than one-third of the entire Asian-American population in the United States now resides in California.

By the end of the decade, our nation's classrooms will be still more diverse, with more Asian-Americans, more African-Americans, and more Hispanics. By the year 2010 there will be 62.5 million school-age children in the United States, of whom nearly 39 percent will be children of color (Hodgkinson, 1989e).

Also by that time, nearly half of all school-age children — 32.3 million — will live in a mere nine states: California, Texas, Florida, New York, New Jersey, Pennsylvania, Illinois, Michigan, and Ohio. Of these 32.3 million children, almost half (15 million) will represent racial or ethnic minorities. In Texas and California, already more than half of school-age children are children of color.

These developments represent unprecedented challenges and opportunities in the field of education. The challenge is to develop a curriculum that embraces the diversity of students and draws upon their various backgrounds as an educational resource. The opportunity is for all children to benefit from the diverse experiences of their peers.

Though the term *diversity*, as applied to students, describes not only race, ethnic origin, religion, physical disability, economic status, and cultural background, in the context of education it most often modifies the last of these: culture. *Culture* is variously defined by anthropologists as the shared values, morals, traditions, and customs that govern the way a group's members construct their beliefs, values, perceptions, and behavior (e.g., Goodenough, 1987). Partaking of a given culture and cultural adaptation, it should be noted, are voluntary.

Sharing in a culture binds its members and permits them to live and function successfully. Members of a cultural group can be identified by life-style, language, and family relationships, to name a few indicators.

There is a vast literature on cultural pluralism — the structure of society that embraces the cultural diversity of individual groups, encourages assimilation into the mainstream, and allows various groups to preserve their ethnic and cultural identities. Cultural pluralism permits people from various ethnic and cultural backgrounds to share in "American culture" and still maintain their ethnic and cultural identities. America's commitment, however, to the values supporting cultural pluralism is not always demonstrated by Americans' behavior. Equal opportunity, for example, is scarcely a reality for all Americans.

Ethnic and racial diversity, unlike cultural diversity, are involuntary. The child of a white family can be racially classified as Caucasian. Ethnically, however, the child's origin could be Irish, German, French, or something else. Racial origin, determined by biology, is often confused with ethnic origin, which is determined by society. Racial classifications include three major groupings: Caucasoid, Mongoloid, and Negroid. A Hispanic — that is, someone of Spanish or Latin American ethnic origin — could actually belong to all three major racial groups (Casanova, 1987).

Ethnicity is involuntary membership in a group with common or shared cultural identification. Ethnic origins can often be blurred by recently arrived immigrants who may wish to be assimilated into the dominant culture. Frequently, nonassimilated groups or those wishing to maintain ties to their countries of origin express their ethnicity through religious or social outlets, such as churches, social clubs, and fraternal organizations. Other groups establish residential enclaves where those denied access to neighborhoods of the dominant culture can maintain a strong ethnic identification. Little Italy in New York City, Chinatown in San Francisco, and Little Saigon in California's Orange County are cases in point.

Social class or socioeconomic status also creates diversity in the classroom. Social class derives from a combination of affluence, influence, income, occupation, and education. In the United States today, owing to household income, 40 percent of the nation's poor are children. Single-parent, female head-of-household families have an average annual income of just over $11,000. Some 15 million American children belong to this category. Nearly 32 percent of all families in the United States earn less than $20,000 a year. Further contributing to the imbalance is the fact that middle-class families of all races are having fewer children (Hodgkinson, 1989e).

Religion can exert a strong influence on the diversity of the educational environment. Both Casanova (1987) and Gollnick and Chinn (1990) note that people of the Jewish faith are frequently termed an ethnic group, owing to their common history. For this group, religion often influences behavior more than country of origin does. A Russian Jew, for example, would likely have more in common with a Jew from Italy or Spain than with a non-Jewish Russian.

In the United States, though religious pluralism is manifest in the wide range of religions practiced, the vast majority of Americans — 90 percent — belong to one of the three dominant faiths: Protestant, Roman Catholic, and Jewish. Despite the First Amendment's separation of church and state and the fact that religious instruction is proscribed in public schools, the influence of religion on education is a fact of American life. (The impact of the Church of Jesus Christ of Latter-day Saints — the Mormons — on educational and curricular matters can be found in schools throughout Utah.)

Religious beliefs continue to stir the emotions of many parents of public school children, and many communities find themselves torn over such issues as sex education, distribution of information on AIDS, the choice of textbooks and other curricular matters. Because American education is essentially controlled by local citizen boards, many elections of school board members and school superintendents are effectively decided by religious groups.

Gender is another component of diversity affecting public schools. Children traditionally learn the social norms appropriate to gender from their families. To repeat, this is learned behavior. Deviance from the norm is not well received, despite American tolerance in general and unisex trends in particular.

Schools also play an important part in the socialization process surrounding gender. Gollnick and Chinn (1990) note that society's values regarding gender roles are deeply embedded in the elementary school curriculum. Teachers accord different kinds of attention to and expect different kinds of behavior from males and females. Gollnick and Chinn's studies indicate that low-achieving boys receive the most negative feedback from teachers and high-achieving boys the most positive feedback; girls, whatever their performance, receive the least feedback of any kind. American society and its public school system are also laboring to eradicate regressive sexual stereotypes that perpetuate inequities and iniquities in the job market — especially for women.

The treatment of the disabled, another diversity subset, mirrors the treatment of oppressed minorities generally. Prior to landmark judicial decisions and federal legislation regarding the right to treatment and the right to education, handicapped children were routinely denied equal educational opportunity. Severely disabled children were often denied access to public education and some were even relegated to state institutions for the mentally retarded.

There has been progress for disabled children, however, from no access at all to education, to access in special schools, to access in regular classrooms for at least part of the school day. What began as an experiment known as mainstreaming became a means of allowing disabled children to learn alongside their able-bodied peers. This experiment later became the cornerstone of the Least Restrictive

Environment (LRE) requirement of Public Law 94-142.

Let us turn now to multicultural education itself. The term *multicultural education* has many meanings. As defined by Gollnick and Chinn (1990), a multicultural education "addresses cultural diversity and equality in schools." Its goals are to promote the strength and value of cultural diversity, to promote human rights and respect for those who are different, to promote alternative life choices, to promote social justice and equality for all, and to promote equity in the distribution of power and income (Gollnick & Chinn, 1990). When we have finally created schools that meet the needs of *all* children, we will have created a truly multicultural education system (Sleeter & Grant, 1988).

Following are some of the benefits to be derived from such an education:

- Children would achieve to their maximum potential, and differences owing to race and gender would disappear.
- Classes would be fully integrated — all tracking would end.
- Teachers would be sensitive to and prepared to deal effectively with diversity.
- Curricula and textbooks would be free of bias and stereotyping.
- Diversity would be something to celebrate, not a "problem" to be remediated.
- Children would be free to think creatively and to explore critically the content to be offered.

Developing a multicultural system of education is the challenge of the 1990s. Teachers able and willing to embrace it could expect such changes as these:

- A curriculum that teaches to and from the specific experiences of the students.
- A climate of high expectation and positive affirmation.
- A curriculum that validates and builds children's self-esteem and a sense of their own culture and national background and, at the same time, broadens their perspectives to incorporate new worlds.
- A physical and social environment that reflects acknowledgment of and excitement about the diversity of its human inhabitants.
- A human relations climate that deliberately and clearly sets norms of acceptable behavior with regard to mutual respect, emotional safety, and appreciation of diversity.
- A pedagogy that emphasizes classroom processes in which students learn from each other through group work and sharing.
- An emphasis upon concept development, verbal and written expression, and communication.
- An emphasis upon developing complex intellectual skills, critical thinking, and analytical tools (Olsen & Mullen, 1990).

When National Educator Award recipients attending this year's retreat were asked to consider approaches for meeting the challenge of diversity in education, their suggestions fell into three categories: curricular modifications, staff development for teachers, and community and parental involvement.

All participants agreed that meeting the instructional needs of diverse students begins with a curriculum and textbooks that are free of bias. Curricular material should be chosen that will increase students' awareness and appreciation of diverse populations, and especially these groups' contributions to American society. Literature rendering differences among groups in a positive light can heighten the self-esteem of minority students. Workshop participants also noted that children from diverse backgrounds can be helped to feel important and integrated into class and school by teachers who tap their experiences and traditions and incorporate them in class activities. The successful teacher will employ a range of educational materials from a variety of cultural, racial, and ethnic groups.

Also mentioned on the curricular front was the so-called seamless fabric approach, which weaves into the curriculum materials of particular relevance to students of varying racial and ethnic backgrounds. Surrounding the curriculum controversy is the tendency of public schools to present a watered-down or "teacher-proof" curriculum. Workshop participants voiced the opinion that educators must have the courage and vision to offer a rigorous curriculum and maintain high expectations for all students.

The use of various cultural holidays, such as Cinco de Mayo, as learning experiences was debated as well. Some educators see such holidays as channels for understanding different students' heritages, for instilling pride in diversity among students, and for celebrating diversity itself. Others, however, are concerned that such separate activities actually fuel racial tensions. Though no consensus was reached, it was generally agreed that establishing some sort of link with diverse students' heritage is important.

Participants agreed that establishing clear rules of social conduct is vital to successful teaching. All students must understand that unfair and hurtful treatment of children from minority cultures or children with disabilities will not be tolerated. A number of educators felt that mere tolerance was an inadequate response to diversity, and that acceptance should be the order of the day. Others noted the need for a "social curriculum" that promotes an understanding of and appreciation for differences. Bridging this critical social gap is crucial to teachers' establishing of sound relations among all students.

Participants were virtually unanimous in their agreement that training in multicultural education is essential for all teachers. The need is all the more imperative as the number of teachers from diverse racial, cultural, and ethnic backgrounds is shrinking while the number of such students is increasing dramatically.

The educators suggested that training in multicultural education include the following elements:

• Understanding of developmental psychology, including learning styles, linguistic development, and so on.

- Appreciation and understanding of the impact of culture and language on learning styles.
- The design of appropriate learning activities and teaching strategies to accommodate differences in learning styles related to culture or language.
- A focus on the positive aspects of all cultures.
- Employment of learning activities that incorporate and capitalize on children's cultural and ethnic heritages.
- Understanding of the nature and impact of disabling conditions on learning and achievement.
- The design of appropriate learning activities and teaching skills to accommodate differences due to disabilities.
- Modeling of appropriate behaviors so that students are exposed to positive role models regarding interaction with diverse students.
- Understanding of the critical importance of teacher expectations for diverse students, especially as they relate to a self-fulfilling prophecy of failure.
- Implementation of instructional materials and strategies designed to enhance students' critical thinking skills, and employment of cooperative learning activities that can have a more positive effect on the achievement of diverse students.

Staff development, of course, is not confined to teachers. Participants felt it critical that all school staff — counselors, custodial staff, cafeteria workers, and bus drivers — be trained in the needs of diverse students. Training for noninstructional staff should focus on issues of cultural sensitivity and the influence of culture, ethnicity, gender, and disability on social skills.

All participants acknowledged the central importance of parent involvement in the education of diverse students. Some even saw the school as potentially the best forum for grasping and meeting the challenges inherent in the changing demographics of today's society. For parents from certain cultures who are unaccustomed to any sort of engagement with their children's schools, this relationship could prove difficult. Social gatherings geared to various cultural holidays and extracurricular activities involving parents and students were suggested as ways to appeal to a possibly reticent older generation.

The community is also a vital resource on which teachers and principals can and must draw as they work to meet the needs of a diverse student body. In fact, more and more educators are seeing that the community's two principal institutions, the school and the place of worship, are the only remaining organizations for coordinating and delivering vital services. A number of participants voiced the belief, moreover, that the community is a mother lode of diverse role models, speakers, and ancillary instructors for educators to tap in the effort to provide multicultural education (Gollnick & Chinn, 1990).

If the community is crucial to the well-being of the school, the converse is equally true, and participants held that it is essential for educators to play a major role in reshaping the public policy agenda. The last decade of school reform, as affected by what Hodgkinson (1989e) terms the "demographic agenda," has been unimpressive: The rate of graduation (from both high school and college) remains flat, poverty among American youth remains high, schools are more sharply segregated for Hispanics today than they were for African-American youth previously, achievement test scores for the lowest third of the school population are static, and "equity" funding has not materialized.

The challenges before American educators and their increasingly diverse student population, though complex and difficult, are not insoluble, provided that educators take the following actions:

- Ensure that *all* children have a "healthy" start through the provision of adequate health care to pregnant women and through early intervention programs such as Head Start.
- Establish high expectations for all children and eradicate the reasons some children currently fail in school.
- Increase the number of diverse youngsters who stay in school and graduate with some salable skills or the preparation for postsecondary education.
- Increase the talent pool of diverse youngsters.
- Aggressively recruit, and then retain, a more diverse teacher work force.
- Recognize that diversity is reality and that it is in the self-interest of all Americans for our nation's schoolchildren to succeed.
- Recognize that multicultural education is not a fad, but a necessity.

Only by making these changes can we hope to nurture and produce the diverse high school graduates for whom serious educators are hoping and planning.

Carolyn L. Ellner

"One of my professors once told me that he had been troubled by a recurrent dream," recounted a participant of the National Educator Awards Retreat. "Each night he would dream that he was being given the secrets of the universe, the secrets of life. When he awoke, however, he could never remember what those secrets were. This bothered him so much that he went to a colleague and told him about it.

"If I were you, said the friend, I would keep a pencil and paper beside my bed and try to force myself into waking from the dream and writing down those secrets of life while they were still fresh in my mind.

"The professor decided to try it. That night he did his best to concentrate on awakening as soon as he began his dream. To his amazement, it worked. In the dream he was given the secrets of life and the universe, and after he had read them he forced himself to awaken. He scribbled on the pad and fell back into a deep sleep. The next morning the professor awoke and reached for the paper. There he knew would be the secrets of life. With trembling hands, he held up the paper and read what he had written. It said: 'Think in other terms.'"

This anecdote describes precisely what the retreat participants were doing generally as they tackled the complex issue of attracting, preparing, and retaining high-quality teachers.

Despite the efforts of some textbook companies and curriculum manufacturers to downplay the importance of teachers by developing so-called teacher-proof materials, the single most important person in the educational system is the teacher. It is the teacher who stimulates and supports students who are brilliant as well as those who are learning at a different pace. It is the good teacher who is the key ingredient in the good school.

It is imperative that there be a supply of high-quality teachers to provide for the increasing number of diverse pupils entering the nation's schools. Most researchers agree that at least 850,000 new teachers are needed in the United States within this decade, both to replace those leaving the profession and to provide for students entering the system. Estimates run as high as 5 million teachers needed in the next five years.

Historically, there have been periodic shortages of teachers, but rarely, if ever, has the challenge been as great as it is today. Children born addicted to drugs are now entering the school system, alongside children from widely diverse backgrounds and cultures. Many have difficulty learning because they are ill or because they cannot speak English. As the expectations of society have changed, so have the expectations for teachers: They are greater. School responsibilities have come to encompass social welfare issues such as poverty, sex education, and drug awareness.

One of the first tasks of the National Educator Award recipients as they studied the issue of attracting high-quality teachers was to determine the characteristics of such educators. Panel members were asked to list the attributes of a good teacher. Many of these qualities are brought to the profession; others are acquired in preparation programs. The attributes listed included energy, humor, patience, sensitivity, broad knowledge of subject matter, flexibility, enthusiasm, creativity, determination, dynamism, empathy, involvement, passion for learning, spontaneity, organization, credibility, and optimism, to name a few.

Retreat participants also agreed that high-quality educators should be strong communicators, risk takers, dreamers, and agents of change, and that they should possess natures that are loving, nurturing, encouraging, and challenging. A list that would be demanding of any professional, this roster also presupposes a basic pedagogical strength.

How can we attract a sizable number of talented college graduates to an occupation that features low wages, poor or tenuous working conditions, waning professional prestige, declining public support, and few opportunities for the exercise of professional judgment?

The literature and the experience of teachers are filled with examples, including horror stories, of the drawbacks of teaching. Teacher compensation has long ranked at or near the bottom of starting salaries for college graduates. Top salaries for experienced teachers rank below those for men and women of equal education and experience in other professions. Today, the average annual salary of a teacher in the United States is $29,000, and starting salaries in some states are lower still.

Just as demoralizing as inadequate salaries are the poor working conditions in many schools. Large classes make the tailoring of the curriculum to the needs of individual students nearly impossible. Not only are textbooks often out of date, there are frequently not enough for all children. Short supplies of such basics as paper, pencils, and chalk are also commonplace.

Teaching can, moreover, be restricting. In many cases teachers are virtual prisoners of the classroom, kept from interacting with other adults or from leaving the classroom for routine activities. Classrooms are often dingy, poorly lit, cold in winter, and hot in summer. Even more serious, violence toward teachers is more common each year. The "blackboard jungle" of the 1950s cinema has become a way of life in many inner-city schools, and teachers and students must rely on police to maintain even a modicum of safety.

In the retreat's first keynote address, Harvard professor Dr. Arthur Levine described what he saw when, as a college president, he arranged to spend a week at a high school in his area. To paraphrase Dr. Levine: Educators, for the most part, were working hard to cope with large, complex, and tenacious problems that were not of their own making. Teachers, who couldn't afford to live on their salaries and had to hold second and sometimes third jobs, often taught students who came to school without enough to eat who were inadequately housed, clothed, and nurtured. Teen pregnancy, drug abuse, and violence were common school realities. Teachers for their part were leaving the classroom in unprecedented numbers. Science, mathematics, and bilingual teachers were almost impossible to hold. Today's schools, according to Dr. Levine, are facing the decline of the family, rising poverty, changing demographics, and a drug explosion, and churches, parents, and traditional youth groups offer less and less support.

Declining occupational prestige is another factor negatively affecting teachers. The schoolteacher has long been on the receiving end of professional derision perpetuated by such stereotypes as television's Miss Brooks and Mr. Peepers. Surveys regarding the prestige accorded various occupations show teaching near the bottom of the list. Teachers themselves are sharply critical of their own profession.

During the 1980s, diminishing public support made a career in teaching increasingly undesirable. The high regard in which the profession was once held — whatever the shortcomings of individual teachers — is a thing of the past. Gallup polls only confirm the trend.

Voucher programs permitting students to take their tax dollars to private schools are finding fervent support among the media and various interest groups. Bond issues to provide new buildings for an exploding student population are routinely defeated. Renovations of run-down buildings are deferred. Legislators committed to preventing new taxes are swept into office. Not satisfied with no-new-tax legislators, pressure groups support the decrease of current taxes. A reverberating outcry has been raised against the state of public education.

The lack of opportunity for teachers to exercise professional judgment reduces the appeal of teaching even more. Administrators and their bureaucratic counterparts generally make most decisions, which are then relayed to teachers who have little recourse but to implement them.

Given these factors, how does public education go about attracting high-quality teachers? Probably the most important strategy is to eliminate these negative factors. Though retreat participants found it difficult to rank the impediments, there was some consensus on their order. First, compensation should be commensurate with the level of a teacher's preparation. Working conditions must be improved. Opportunities to plan and to reflect must be built into the teacher's day. The teacher must feel physically safe in his or her classroom. Teachers need to be directly involved in school management. And finally, the status of teachers must be improved. To do all this, a campaign to change the public image of teaching must be aggressively waged.

Retreat participants held that the process of teacher recruitment must start early and continue with financial, professional, and emotional support for the potential recruit. "Future Teacher" clubs formed as early as elementary school are a place to start. These would allow children to increase their awareness of the educational process. Playing the role of teacher, students in the upper grades could tutor younger children. Such clubs in junior and senior high schools could have their own appeal, as peer teaching at this level can be a sound introduction to the profession. Serving as teacher aides in the senior year of high school and as teacher assistants in the early college years are also valuable experiences for prospective teachers.

Accompanying this early experience should be financial support permitting bright students from low-income families — and especially minority representatives — to survive the expense of college. The current practice of forgiving the loans of teacher candidates is inadequate for keeping candidates in teacher preparation programs. Scholarships, grants, and internships are the strategies of choice.

As important as early experience and financial backing is emotional support. Peers can provide a measure of this support, as can mentors such as recent graduates, professors, or other classroom teachers. Career and personal counseling should be available to anyone who needs it.

Retreat panelists repeatedly invoked the formulation that the product cannot be better than the ingredients used to produce it. Thus, whatever the method of recruitment, the greatest effort must be made to encourage top students to go into teaching. The profession needs the best and the brightest, not only among those just reaching adulthood, but also among mature men and women who have succeeded in other professions and are looking for career change and new challenges. We need university professors to urge the best students to consider teaching as a career.

The most effective recruitment strategy is for teachers to recruit new teachers. Students can be galvanized by individual teachers, who can be an example and an inspiration *if* they share their enthusiasm with their students. When likely candidates are identified, instructors should be encouraging, offering them concrete reasons they would be good teachers. Teachers must also communicate pride in their profession, and students must be aware of it from kindergarten. In short, teachers must be role models for the next generations.

One retreat educator put forth the following questions as goals for student recruitment to the ranks of teaching:

- What if every teacher were encouraged to talk directly about the rewards of teaching with those students who show intelligence and caring and the potential to be good teachers?
- What if we used teachers who are recognized for excellence to serve as guest speakers to recruit future teachers at career fairs, at school assemblies, or in classrooms?

- What if we identified our most promising minority students and paid them to work with students in classrooms, where they would experience the joy of working with children and recognize the personal rewards that can come only from the teaching profession?
- What if we established "Future Teacher" clubs in which students would be involved in projects that would direct them toward careers in education?

If these queries were taken out of the realm of speculation and put into practice, we would see a real advance toward the development of high-quality teachers.

Most teachers are not born; they are made. Students need to know that there is a body of knowledge that precedes the professional educator. They need to know that there is a theoretical basis — supported by a foundation of research — to teaching. Teachers need to know that they can *acquire* a philosophy to underpin their practice, that there *are* teaching options from which to choose, that they can *develop* the skill of making reasoned choices and of tailoring their teaching to their students' needs. Much of this they will learn in college and in their preservice programs. More of it they will develop later in the classroom with students.

As teachers, we must remember our own times of struggle, and as we do we must remind the novice that it takes strength to teach what one believes in, and that it takes more than one educational avenue to lead today's students to success. We must demonstrate for these men and women that there are ways of teaching that are genuinely exciting, ways of using reasoning and modifying classroom structures that allow a teacher to make lasting contact with a student. We must also help prospective teachers develop the resources and materials that will allow them to build their curricula.

Retreat participants' suggestions for improving teacher preparation asked for *more* of what they have: more direct experience with a wider variety of students, more economic support for the teacher candidate, more opportunities for using technology, more discussion of and practice in classroom and school management, more emphasis on subject matter, more strategies for teaching, and, finally, more orientation to reality in teacher preparation programs.

Some participants held that methodology should be taught in the public schools, where it is, after all, to be applied, rather than only at the university level. In fact, many participants felt that *all* course work should be taught in the schools themselves. Future teachers must cultivate a variety of perspectives and be exposed to a variety of work environments before taking charge of their own classrooms.

The role of the master teacher, specially trained for the task of inducting new recruits to the profession, underscores the imperative for trainees to work with the best teachers available.

The necessity of improving preservice income points to such programs as paid internships that allow trainees to participate in the entire public school schedule. Earlier assistance might include credit for experience as a paid classroom aide.

Scholarships and loan forgiveness, of course, offer other means of economic assistance. Year-round schools also offer aspiring and new teachers the chance to moonlight by being substitute teachers in their "off-track" time.

Because the teachers of tomorrow must be versed in the use of computers, video technology, and interactive television, we must expose them to the most current teaching techniques. Videotaped lessons can be a useful tool for self-improvement, computers can enrich the curriculum and individualize instruction, and interactive television can make teaching and learning more exciting for everyone involved.

Management training should include the acquisition not only of administrative skills but also of skills that promote professional interaction and engender greater autonomy. School-based management has proven effective, but teachers working with other school constituents need to be part of that management also, and in the process they must be treated as professionals. Giving more responsibility to teachers not only spurs pride, it develops real managerial skills.

In the effort to develop greater teacher competence in given subjects higher standards (such as a certain grade average) should be considered. Requiring passing grades on standard subject-matter exams could also be effective.

Retreat participants considered it of particular importance that all university professors — not only those in schools of education — be models of good pedagogy, and that, toward this end, they be encouraged to reflect on their own teaching.

Studies have shown that as many as 25 percent of new teachers leave the profession within their first year, and that 50 percent of new teachers quit within five years. Considering the cost in time and money to teacher candidates and the institutions that recruit and prepare them, good public policy dictates practices that will help keep new teachers in the profession.

The California State Legislature recognized this imperative when it accorded joint authorization to the Commission on Teacher Credentialing and the State Department of Education to establish New Teacher Projects to determine the most beneficial supports and assessments. It is expected that when the projects report their findings, the legislature will make new teacher support and assessment a part of the credentialing system.

A Retreat participant from Connecticut noted some of that state's strategies to retain teachers. Connecticut's strategy maintains that the training of teachers should provide novice teachers the opportunity to work with mentors who have been specifically trained to help them through the first-year or two of teaching. The state's BEST and Mentor programs tap the expertise of veteran teachers to do just that. Using their knowledge and skills, veterans help prepare novice teachers for the profession by serving as cooperating teachers to college students doing their "student teaching," by serving as mentors to first-year teachers, or by serving as assessors who administer processes leading to certification.

Furthermore, in order to maintain and retain teachers, Connecticut's strategy is to have programs that recognize and reward teachers for their ability, creativity, and leadership. The state finds that these programs are not only gratifying to the veterans, they provide incentives to continue creating innovative and successful methods of instruction.

The Connecticut programs have lifted the spirits of many veterans by making them feel part of the preparation of the next generation of teachers. Veteran teachers need programs that provide opportunities for them to grow professionally, to share their knowledge, and to continue to be lifetime learners.

Among retreat participants' suggestions for improving teacher retention, improvement of professional status figured most prominently. Though increased compensation was noted as an inducement to stay in the profession, studies have indicated that new teachers are fully aware of the low salary factor, and that the problem lies elsewhere.

A sustained communication effort geared to elevating the status of the profession is considered one workable means to improve new teacher retention. This could well include a commitment by the media to cover education fully and fairly — that is to say, to cover its strengths as well as its weaknesses. Teacher recognition programs were also suggested, especially those established by businesses.

Working conditions are an obvious factor in any employee's decision to keep or quit his or her post. For teachers, the most significant aspect of working conditions is the size of the classes they are expected to teach and manage. The amount of time required outside of class (to organize, prepare, and communicate with colleagues) is also considered a significant drawback, as is the underlying lack of job security generated by the financial instability of many school districts.

Retreat participants expressed the concern that beginning teachers need the continuing attention of the universities from which they have received their credentials, as well as the support of the school districts of which they are newly a part. An early assessment procedure was suggested as a means of determining early in their careers those areas in which new teachers need ongoing support and instruction.

New teacher support programs would not only help new teachers' morale, they would create a professional structure spanning the preprofessional and professional experiences. Indeed, a priority budgetary items for any educational institution should be its in-service teacher training program. Little use can be made of all the modern educational resources available if a teacher cannot teach well.

Because today's teachers are the models for tomorrow's, we must do all we can to equip them to teach knowledgeably, creatively, and wholeheartedly. Toward achieving this end, retreat participants posed the following questions:

- What if we made it a daily priority to publicize teachers' accomplishments so that the public might hear firsthand about the successes of American education?
- What if we were to encourage others to recognize and honor teachers for their jobs well done?

- What if we were to encourage parents and students to write to those teachers who had a sound and lasting influence on their lives?
- What if we made it a goal to build the confidence and esteem of teachers so that they might transmit these to their students?
- What if the public were to *demand* that their states' governors, legislatures, and boards of education do something concrete to raise teacher salaries?

The participants of the National Educator Awards Retreat concluded that it is possible to recruit outstanding teachers, to prepare them, and to keep them in the profession, but it takes the committed involvement of elementary, secondary, and higher schools of education, of the business community, and of the public generally. Professionals must talk with lay people; teachers must talk with parents; administrators must talk with businesspeople. And as they do, they all must "think in other terms."

HOW SHOULD OUR SCHOOLS BE STRUCTURED? A VIEW FROM THE TOP OF THE BOTTOM OF THE HEAP

9

Guilbert C. Hentschke

Opinions on how schools should be structured, or restructured, are diverse and described in a range of ways — from terms as simplistic as *choice, basics,* and *power to the schools,* to strategies as complex as those put forth in *A Nation Prepared: Teachers for the 21st Century* (Carnegie Forum on Education and the Economy, 1986). Clearly, the question, How should our schools be structured? is too broadly conceived. A more useful form of this question might be: How do some of the very best teachers and principals think our schools should be structured for our graduates to acquire the strengths and capacities we want them to have? A subtext to this query could be, What do we want our graduates to be like as a consequence of attending American schools?

Although National Educator Award's Retreat workshops produced no single definition of school structures, their participants offered a coherent composite picture of the schooling necessary to bring forth graduates with the qualities we seek. Many of the structural changes recommended addressed the use of the scarcest of all teacher commodities: time. Participants start from the premise that they have much more to do than time allows, but that much can be (and has been) done to rearrange time more productively for teachers. Changes in the allocation of time, however, are often substitutes for desired changes in professional practices.

Professional practices are, in fact, the heart of the issue. Not surprisingly, a number of subsets arrange themselves under such a broad heading: definitions of roles and of authority, for example, intraschool governance, and the need for cooperative working relationships between teachers and professionals in complementary institutions.

The suggested changes in school structures — however disparate — formed a coherent whole. While the workshops' educators believed they could effect most of these changes without great difficulty, it was noted that patience and the support of the profession generally were crucial to the endeavor.

The arguments were coherent in the following sense: If all of the suggestions for restructuring were implemented in the schools of these very good teachers, then these very good teachers would be even more effective. In a different respect, the arguments sometimes put forth for restructuring schools are much more radical than those proposed by the Retreat participants. There are many issues associated with school restructuring that the educators did not dwell on or, in some cases, even mention. There was, for example, no discussion of market-based or performance-based compensation systems, elimination of tenure, public and private school choice, peer review and assistance, or parental accountability.

We should not be surprised that these very good teachers did not recommend radical structural changes in schooling. They were asked to recommend changes in school structures that would be most productive for *them*, not what would be most productive for the entire field or for the average teacher. While the recommendations contained in this chapter probably go a long way toward improving the effectiveness of the already effective, dedicated, and experienced teacher, it does not necessarily follow that they are sufficient to improve the education of the vast majority of our students.

What, then, is restructuring? Consider the following from American Federation of Teachers President Albert Shanker (1990):

Our persistent educational crisis shows that we've reached the limits of our traditional model of education ... we can expect neither greater efficiency nor more equity from our education system ... there seems to be widespread agreement that we must do things differently in our schools ... experience has taught me that, when diverse groups of people start using the same new word or phrase (e.g. restructuring) there is usually not much happening (p. 344).

Restructuring connotes a loosely assembled collection of concepts having to do with the organization and operation of schools. Like many catchphrases, it means different things to different people.

Various concepts, rendered in shorthand terms, have quickly evolved and been appended, not always helpfully, to the idea of restructuring. Examples include school-based management, shared decision making, teacher or parent empowerment, performance-based instruction, authentic assessment, parent choice, teaching for understanding, higher-order thinking, teacher or parent accountability, and "defining education in relation to the customer," to name only a few.

The alleged problems to which these terms attach span the entire landscape of the profession. They include ill-conceived multiple-choice tests, misuse of test results, autocratic principals, the insensitivity of district representatives to teachers and of teachers to parents, rules geared to processes, and U.S. students' poor performance vis-à-vis their foreign counterparts.

If the issue of school structuring generates new issues and vocabulary, it is also prompting scholarly efforts to synthesize the many parts of the problem. In *Restructuring Schools: Capturing and Assessing the Phenomena*, for example, Murphy and Evertson (in press) identify a variety of factors that have led to school restructuring. They link these factors to "effects" such as work redesign, governance structures, and "authority flows" in schools.

One depiction of school restructuring, offered by Marc Tucker, has the virtues of integrity and brevity. First elaborated in *A Nation Prepared: Teachers for the 21st Century* (Carnegie Forum on Education and the Economy, 1986) and subsequently refined in *Restructuring Education* (National Center on Education and the Economy, 1990, p. 10), Tucker's tract provides the cornerstone for current school restructuring efforts in many school districts around the country. According to the author, the many discrete elements of school restructuring boil down to seven guiding principles that themselves issue from three related themes.

The first theme addresses the issue of what we expect from an education. The idea is to assess students' actual performance in relation to what we hope they will accomplish; that is, to establish "student performance standards." Put differently, the idea is to focus on how students come out, not how they got where they were going, and on outcomes, less than on processes.

The second theme is to make sure that those closest to students — that is, teachers and administrators — should be topflight professionals, a notion that flies in the face of the reality that the positions of teacher and principal tend to be the least important in the profession. The standard measures of professional accomplishment, such as salary, authority, and the ability to change professional practices or achieve more recognition, all increase in relation to the distance maintained between educator and educated. Inverting this arrangement is implicit in restructuring the school.

The third theme concerns initiating incentives for outstanding educators to educate their students to certain "performance standards." The outstanding educator is willing to be held accountable for student performance in exchange for increased control over the modes of education.

This description of the structure of public schooling not only fundamentally departs from the case in schools as we know them, it also accords with the process of identifying outstanding teachers and principals (such as National Educator Award recipients) and asking them (a) What do we want our graduates to be like? and (b) What changes in school structures would be most conducive to educating such students?

Before we can discuss restructuring, let us consider the structure as it is. The essential difference between the structure as it is and how restructuring would have it is the difference between uniformity/stasis and variety/innovation. R.F. Elmore (1987) depicts the former "one-size-fits-all" school as having six "continuities of professional practice":

- The day is divided into units of time, each of which is assigned a specific subject to be taught. Content may vary from day to day according to school scheduling practice, the teacher's pace of instruction, and unanticipated interruptions.

- In each unit of time, a single teacher works with a particular group of children in a single classroom.
- The teacher's work is defined almost entirely in terms of the time spent with students.
- "Whole-group" instruction takes precedence over individual instruction.
- Instruction is initiated by the teacher, and teacher instruction is the dominant communication.
- Knowledge is defined in terms of mastery of received information.

These practices, the most visible elements of school operating structures, are driven by a combination of state regulation, school board policy, union contracts, and "tradition," which, together, form the structure of American public schools.

This form of school structure is related to educators' position on the lowest rung of the career ladder. It is precisely because teachers and principals occupy the bottom two levels of the professional pyramid of education that directives about course content and the like issue from the top down. Rules and regulations are promulgated and enforced by middle- and upper-level managers to ensure that a required process of education is carried out. While this pyramid may have functioned productively earlier in the century, today it is the problem in education. Hence, the imperative for restructuring.

Although variations on the restructuring theme are frequently heard among governmental, educational, and business leaders, one rarely hears the views of educational practitioners on this subject. As the very best of these (including National Educator Award recipients) are truly committed to and talented at implementing the directives issued from above, and as it is they who would be implementing the restructured practices, it is fitting that we seek their views on what most needs to be changed in the organization and operation of our schools.

The sweeping nature and vague definition of "structure" notwithstanding, National Educator Award recipients had no reticence whatever about naming the structural changes most needed for producing the high school graduates we want. Four changes — to be effected simultaneously — emerged from discussions with these educators:

1. They would change — and in many cases have already changed — the use of time.
2. They would set in motion a wide range of promising new professional practices.
3. As a means to points 1 and 2, they would reorder relationships of authority and redefine certain roles within the school.
4. They would make similar rearrangements of roles and responsibilities with regard to educators and the outside community of parents, labor unions, institutions of higher education, social service agencies, and the central office.

Although the main thrust of restructuring is toward student achievement, the issue of time and all its ramifications figured prominently in the educators' thinking. As one put it: "We [teachers] are all bound up in schedules and 'class times,' and there is no time to do anything. Students also are ruled by 'seat time.' We should [all] be pursuing achievement, not merely passing time."

For all their variety, the suggestions on the use and misuse of time in every case departed from the traditional and uniform mode of five-period days, five-day weeks, and nine-month years. Some examples include proposals for a longer school year, time for parent visits, a longer school day, more flexible allocation of time, more time for children to be in school without teachers, and time for staff development. These suggestions are neither random nor at odds with one another. Rather, they constitute a remarkably coherent picture of what the restructured school should be like with respect to time.

The call for students to spend more time in school goes beyond recognizing that American students spend considerably less time in school than many of their foreign counterparts from industrialized nations. It has more to do with the daily and weekly rhythm of American schooling. For a number of educators, a change in this pattern has meant opening school earlier in the morning and closing it later in the afternoon so that school can be a place for playing as well as for learning. This kind of extended time would also provide more time for students to get to know their teachers outside of class.

Many teachers feel that because their entire schedule is geared toward class instruction they lack the time necessary to perform important tasks that when left undone greatly reduce the effectiveness of even brilliant classroom teaching. Additional time for teachers would also afford them the chance to learn more about their students and to calibrate their courses accordingly.

Teachers would use a good part of the extra time they seek to interact with other adults, namely, other teachers, parents, and social service agency professionals. Even the best classroom instruction can be seriously undermined if it is not reinforced by the other adults in a student's life.

The educators' discussion concerning the need for more time to communicate with parents had more to do with wanting to help parents understand the importance of providing proper conditions for children's learning than with their paying more visits to school. The issue also arose of teachers visiting parents in the home — a very time-consuming enterprise.

Though there are many ways to achieve more productive use of time, retreat participants rated uniform or mandated changes as among the least effective. Rather, because the use of time is so idiosyncratic, they felt that there likely is no one best solution as to its disposition. Furthermore, the educators thought that whatever solutions are put forth should come from the local level. Indeed, the use of time should be under continuous review at individual schools.

Workshop participants acknowledged that extra time can be gained in a number of ways. One teacher reported that by adding 10 minutes to each class her school acquired an extra day per month for teachers to work among themselves. Another indicated that the addition of 15 minutes to each class yielded an extra hour per week for similar teacher meetings. Another school has four long days of classes, with the fifth day "free," giving students the chance to be in school for recreation with volunteers rather than in class with teachers.

Certain alterations in the allocation of time can properly be determined only at the district or state level. For example, ideally, there would be a longer school year, since, as one educator put it, "It is unfair to compare what we do in 180 days with what teachers in other countries do in 250 days." Given more days, however, workshop participants would not simply "do more of the same." Indeed, recommendations for concrete changes in professional practice were fundamental and far-reaching.

As Smylie and Denny (1989) put it, "The development of new roles for teachers [is] on the crest of the wave of restructuring" (p. 236). One district describes its changes as follows:

> Lead Teachers, Teacher-Directors, and Teacher-Coordinators are a growing part of the ... landscape. Lead Teachers now supervise the program's operation in cooperation with their host school's principal. Lead Teachers teach classes; but they also perform appropriate administrative/supervisory duties on a day-to-day basis, while remaining part of the teachers' bargaining unit ... [Teacher Directors are] exclusively responsible for the programs they direct (Dade County Public Schools, 1989, p. 11).

Increased time is a means to the end, not the end itself. It makes possible activities that were previously impossible and establishes as a norm certain practices that under the old arrangement only the most exceptional educators would have found the time for.

It is increasingly difficult and vital for teachers to engage more closely with parents. Closer contact can allow the teacher to gain better understanding of the student's home environment, to assist parents in the education of their children, and to aid the parent in finding noneducation outside assistance, should it be necessary.

Many different parent involvement activities were discussed by the workshop participants. One school offers child care for parents when they visit school. Another has created a Family Resource Center that provides a variety of information and services for parents and children. With or without such resources, many participants feel that one of the most effective ways of reaching their students is through the visits they pay to parents at home.

National Educator Award recipients attach a great deal of importance to their own professional development, yet among all educators, teachers are the least likely to have either the time or the financial resources to do so. What little time they do have for staff development is consumed by other educators' ideas of how they should be developing themselves.

National Educator Award recipients have broken the time-constraint mold and initiated a number of ingenious practices for furthering their own professional development. Some have established professional "leave banks" where substitute time is "banked" and "drawn down," enabling teachers to take time out from school for professional development activities and later fill in for others as they take their time off. Other teachers have developed their own "educational issues forums" where teachers take turns leading group discussions on various development topics. In still another district, teachers have made a compact with a nearby university to exchange services; for example, the teachers can take university courses free of charge in exchange for supervising student teachers. Of particular interest to teachers are courses that discuss methodologies that foster the independence and critical thinking of students.

When teachers have more time they can work more with each other. The old model of one teacher with one class for one year is crumbling. Some teachers are now working in groups and assuming collective responsibility for educating their students over a two- or three-year period. Implicit in the new model is the requirement of more time for teachers to work together. The positive impact on the student of such a sustained relationship with the teacher is considerable.

There are, of course, many issues beyond considerations of time. The traditional process of "teacher evaluation" is being transformed in a number of ways. Teachers are assuming the responsibility of mentoring and providing guidance to probationary teachers. Many others are simply helping their colleagues in whatever ways arise.

Some of the retreat participants are changing the ways they assess the achievement of their students. Instead of relying solely on multiple-choice, norm-referenced tests, teachers are also considering student portfolios containing essays, experiment results, and the like. Teachers see at least two benefits from this shift: Portfolio contents offer more concrete evidence than tests alone can of whether or not the student is on the track of being "what we want our graduates to be like," and portfolio contents actually indicate what the student has learned — information crucial for real student and teacher assessment. Contrast this with the inherent limitations of standardized tests that test all students in a grade each year, compare incomparable groups of students, and report test results months late.

Carnoy and MacDonnell (1990) have referred to school restructuring as "governance or management reform" (p. 51). According to Chubb (1988):

> The more control a school has over those aspects of its organization that affect its performance — the articulation of goals, the selection and management of teachers, the specification of policies — the more likely it is to exhibit the qualities that have been found to promote effectiveness (p. 38).

Changes in the professional practices of teachers do not occur in a vacuum, and this is especially true of changes in the ways principals and teachers interact. As one researcher has put it, "The relationship between teachers and principals is at the crux of school restructuring" (Rallis, 1990, p. 189). Changes in the use of time assume changes in professional practices, which in turn suggest changes in roles and authority in the school. Who, for example, has the authority to determine the schedule of the day, of the week, of the year? Who allocates scarce financial resources? Who decides how students will be grouped? Who determines the use of time? National Educator Award recipients suggest that many of these decisions are best made at the school level, which raises the question of who, within the school structure, should make them.

While acknowledging that the principal is ultimately responsible for the operation of a school, and indeed is a critical factor in the success of a school, National Educator Awards Retreat participants — including principals — stressed the importance and efficacy of group decision making and collective responsibility. The aim goes beyond involving teachers in decisions normally made by principals unilaterally; it also extends to decisions in which neither teachers nor principals have traditionally had a major voice.

The teachers and principals taking part in retreat workshops have been making fundamental instructional decisions in their schools. They have been creating "schools within schools," for instance; they have pursued various waivers of state and federal regulations and local union contracts; they have changed staffing patterns within their schools when they felt such changes would benefit students; and, increasingly, they have served on committees (which occasionally have included parents) that decide on the deployment of financial resources.

In addition to sharing management tasks, several principals indicated that they themselves have direct contact — either as teachers or as counselors — with students. One principal described being a roving substitute teacher, thus freeing up teachers for nonroutine assignments.

Sharing responsibilities in this way requires open and frank communication among teachers and on-site administrators, which in turn promotes mutual accountability. Many educators are seeking assessment as a group rather than as individuals; they are moving from a notion of: Is the teacher teaching well? to: What are teachers doing for the children? This sort of shift is likely to improve teachers' abilities as well as provide a better perspective from which to view their behavior. And although student achievement should not be the only criterion for judging teachers' effectiveness, teachers are trying to keep better track of students' progress.

The criterion for measuring principals' success is also changing. Today, the question principals have to answer to is, What is the administrator doing to enhance the effectiveness of teachers in the classroom?

Let us turn our attention now to the role of relationships outside the school house. As Finn (1991) has pointed out:

Huge territory ... is inhabited by the individuals, agencies, organizations and services that dominate the 91 percent of youngsters' live spent outside school. The responsibility for educating the next generation does not belong only to teachers and principals ... even if we succeed in obliging the average child to spend a significantly larger portion of his young life attending school ... the out-of-school part is unlikely to fall below 85 percent, (p. 306, 352).

Restructuring cannot be achieved by teachers and site administrators alone. Although, as we have seen, ground-breaking steps can be profitably taken, restructuring by definition requires changes in the behavior of other key figures, such as parents, educators based outside of school, and representatives from other professions serving the needs of children.

Further, although it is clear enough that parents should be actively engaged with their children's schools, workshop participants agreed that parental involvement is more effective in the area of children's education than in that of school governance, where parents' newfound authority is liable to be galling, if not threatening, to seasoned educators.

Central-office educators, teacher union officials, and teacher educators play what may seem contradictory parts. Since changes in professional practice and school governance seldom occur without the central participation of district administrators, these groups are key to developing the kinds of structural changes discussed above. On the other hand, such changes shift authority, responsibility, and ultimately schooling decisions directly into the schools — away from the district office, away from the bargaining table, and away from the university. In short, such non-school-based educators will develop more collaborative relationships with educators in schools.

Finally, those from other professions serving the needs of children are developing formal relationships with educators for the sake of improved education and well-being of students. Specialists bringing projects in the fine arts and the humanities to the schools are profiting from extra school time, health officials are scheduling meetings in schools, and various social service agencies are promoting their services to families through the schools.

National Educator Award recipients definitely have a vision of the sorts of revised structures that are conducive to educating "the graduates we want." The vision includes the issues of time, of professional practices, of site-based authority, of shared accountability for student achievement, and of outside influences. Just as important, these teachers and principals have a vision of the kinds of educators who are likely to produce such graduates: those with the very traits of integrity and inquisitiveness they hope to foster in their students.

The models for restructured schools that evolved from discussions with the National Educator Award recipients are unusual and "special" in the sense that all or even most of the good ideas and practices suggested exist in toto in very few, if any, schools. This is to be expected, because the contributors of these ideas are themselves unusual — that is, unusually dedicated, effective educators. It is important for us to listen to and understand what these people have to say about restructuring schools, because they are recognized as among the very best practitioners in schools.

Does it automatically follow that these particular ideas for restructuring schools are sufficient or even the necessary minimum for all educators and schools in the United States? The answer is probably not, for several reasons. First, interesting discussions, even over several days, and even among experts, simply do not permit sufficient exploration in depth of the issue. Taken as first approximations of the most visible issues, the ideas generated stand up well, but not as an exhaustive, comprehensive analysis. The scope of the solution requires complexity beyond what can be discussed in two days and reported in one chapter. Issues of student performance assessment and educator accountability, for example, were barely touched on, despite their central importance in restructuring.

Second, and more fundamental, is the limited nature of the very premise of this chapter: that by asking very highly regarded teachers and principals what changes they value most we can deduce what changes ought to be considered throughout elementary-secondary schooling. It does not necessarily follow that what makes these extraordinarily effective educators even more effective will also work for the "average" educator in an "average" school — that is, for the majority of schools. More to the point, many of the restructuring changes being practiced by these award-winning educators were "coming out of their hides." It simply does not follow that less motivated, less energetic teachers would be equally likely to take up these good ideas. Strategies that have succeeded in addressing problems in one classroom (or school) may not be appropriate policy tools for addressing problems faced in most classrooms (or schools).

Consider as one example the idea that teachers should have more time to work and communicate with other teachers, presumably, but not necessarily, with the same amount of time being spent on teaching children. It is widely accepted that this change would have major benefits for those teachers who feel the need to do meet with and learn from their peers, and who would in fact do so if provided with the opportunity. However, this would arguably not be the case with all teachers, or maybe even with the majority of current teachers. To restructure the vast majority of schools so that teachers will have much more time to work with each other would require much more than rearranging the school week, as has been done in some of the schools of the National Educator Award recipients.

Even assuming that the scope and scale of restructured schools can be brought into existence, there is no inherent guarantee that the desired results will accrue. Restructured schools are the product of society's presumption and hope that the education levels of the vast majority of America's children can be significantly raised beyond current levels. The proof of this lies somewhere in the future.

The restructuring efforts of retreat participants provide important insights into what all schools can become for children and their families. These efforts also serve as testimony to the notion that the structures of schooling can be changed in ways that will improve our chances of getting more graduates with the skills and abilities that we seek. Actually bringing about a society where children are significantly more educated than they are currently will require the sincere efforts of leaders throughout society; very effective teachers and principals, however hardworking and determined they are, will never be able to achieve this goal by themselves.

Harry Handler

Responding to the issue of process assessment, participants in National Educator Awards Retreat workshops concentrated on two themes: the limitations of current approaches to assessing the cognitive and affective behavior of students and the potential of what are currently referred to as "performance-based" or "authentic" approaches to assessment.

Consideration of the following processes was suggested as a starting point for discussion: cognitive processes of students, processes related to student attitudes and behavior, and processes related to school governance and structure. Both the suggested readings and the participants' comments concentrated on the first two points. *Process* refers to several aspects of assessment, including content, format, development, and use of test results. The breadth of interpretation of the term may reflect the inadequacy of the multiple-choice format.

While it was understood that the concept of assessment is much broader than that of testing, there was considerable debate among the retreat participants on the limitations of current norm-referenced, standardized testing programs, or, as some termed them, "multiple-guess tests." Retreat educators were concerned that such tests have a number of shortcomings. They skew the curriculum toward the teaching of those materials (basic skills and individual facts) most easily tested and scored by machine. They carry disproportionate weight and can lead to improper tracking of students. They can block equal access to learning opportunities. They are highly dependent on a knowledge of Standard English and reading and test-taking skills. They are biased in relation to culture, race, and gender. Such tests neither measure what teachers teach nor include teachers in the test development process as a means of aligning local curriculum and assessed objectives. They cut into available teaching time. They impose the imperatives of an "assessment-driven curriculum" when used as part of an accountability system, as they determine what is to be taught. At present, they fail to measure such important skills as critical thinking or creativity and hence yield a narrow (inaccurate) picture of students' talent and schools' efficacy. And they yield results that do not reflect the variety or depth of a comprehensive curriculum.

Retreat participants' concerns paralleled Baker's (1990) criticism of the validity of the measure itself, the influence of tests on teaching and learning, and the accuracy of judgments rendered on the educational system based on such tests. Overall, these tests measure only a narrow band of student performance; encourage superficial thinking, quick answers, and rigid instruction; and constitute highly inadequate devices for assessing the quality of education.

Many retreat educators shared Baker's concern over the use of such tests in the assessment of educational quality. As one participant noted, "The Wall Chart approach is part of a Microwave Assessment Process: A picture is taken once or twice a year of education; it is analogous to a baseball player's salary being determined on some statistic taken once or twice a year."

It is essential to use an approach that provides ongoing assessment. "Snapshot" assessments provide a complete picture of neither a school's effectiveness nor a child's abilities. Such broad-brush assessments simply fail to identify significant individual differences. Annual norm-referenced tests are, moreover, frequently misused by the news media to distinguish "good" and "bad" school systems. Whether the aim is to evaluate individual student achievement or the efficacy of educational programs, ongoing testing in a variety of areas is necessary for a complete and accurate assessment on which to base decisions for effective change.

It is of value to consider certain past concerns that led to the development of current approaches to testing. Previously, research indicated that test results were less than reliable owing to the difficulties of scoring essay tests, hence the development of current approaches, many of which found strong support because they were thought to be objective and because the methods of administration and scoring were standardized. The multiple-choice format was seen as a means of assessing vast amounts of information in a short period of time and at a reasonable cost.

On the basis of additional experience and research, opinions about both of these concerns have changed. The success that many schools, districts, and states have had with the use of "writing samples" appears to have reduced concern over the reliability of scoring. Retreat participants, furthermore, disputed the worth of basing assessment on a mastery of arbitrarily assembled individual facts. The teachers and administrators were more concerned about the deep understanding of subject matter than about broad and superficial content coverage. Given the application of technology, the increase in specialization, and the extraordinary expansion of our knowledge base, the current approach to the testing of knowledge levels appears to have lost whatever intellectual merit or credibility it may once have had. It is simply not possible to know all the facts. Even if it were, theorists now hold that students learn best when facts are taught within a relevant context rather than in an arbitrary sequence, and they believe that information should be assessed in a real-world setting.

Retreat participants expressed interest in and support for the mastery of a number of skills and behaviors that are not readily assessed by norm-referenced, multiple-choice tests. These included the traditional basic skills, but there was also strong support for the development of problem-solving skills, intra- and interpersonal skills, sensitivity to multicultural issues, and "altruistic responsibility." All of these must be assessed if we are to evaluate fairly the effectiveness of schools and the achievements of students.

Retreat educators recognized the need to consider assessment in the context of the retreat theme, "What do we want our graduates to be like?" and as they did so, they bore in mind the following questions:

1. What indicators should be used to determine whether future graduates possess the skills and attitudes of "the graduates we want?"
2. Since many of these indicators are likely to be highly subjective, what should educators do to gain business community support for their use?
3. Can performance-based or authentic approaches to assessment be used effectively as part of a national assessment program focusing on national standards?

As a preface to the participants' responses to these questions, let us consider a number of common themes. There was strong sentiment that educators had been passed over in the process of determining the best assessment methods. The retreat educators expressed the strong belief that the very teachers who deliver the instruction and who depend on assessment results to improve or expand instruction should play a key role in assessment design. For teachers to play this role, time must be made available to them for active involvement in the assessment process and in the development of policies governing student assessment and the standards against which districts and schools are measured.

If we are serious about expanding our methods of determining what students have learned, college and university preservice and in-service training programs demand radical restructuring and improvement. Implementing new assessment programs, particularly those based on performance, will require much instruction for teachers. We must also win greater community support for teachers' "professional judgment." Ascher (1990, p. 21) reports that innovations in testing and instruction go hand-in-glove with the issue of teacher professionalism. Any initiative to impose particular assessment methods should be evaluated according to its likely effect on teacher professionalism. A variety of performance-based or authentic approaches to assessment found strong support among retreat participants. While there will remain a limited role for norm-referenced, standardized, short-answer and multiple-choice tests, it is thought that their overall influence should be significantly reduced. Portfolios, videos, projects, group work, oral presentations, daily journals, hands-on performance, and self-evaluation were just a few of the assessment techniques discussed. Participants noted that each of these techniques can provide unique bits of information about a student's intellectual growth and development. When taken as a whole, these assessment results provide rich, detailed personal portraits of our students.

Data from standardized, multiple-choice tests allow us to understand only a portion of what children know. Results from highly varied, ongoing assessment programs will allow us to understand not only the depth and breadth of students' information stores but also more about how they learn, how they feel about their work, how they approach problem solving, how they integrate knowledge from various content areas, and a host of other learning dimensions.

Educational systems and practices can be no better than our understanding of them. Problems that go unrecognized will remain uncorrected. Strengths that are unseen are unlikely to be reinforced or tapped. A commitment to excellence in education must be a commitment to the development of dynamic, varied assessment programs.

Regarding the first of the three underlying questions raised by retreat participants — that is, "Which indicators should be used to determine whether future graduates possess the skills and attitudes of "the graduates we want?" — the following list of indicators could be employed to assess the affective learning and beliefs of students:

- The number of students who become active volunteers in programs to improve a community's quality of life.
- The number of students who become involved in community recycling programs.
- The reduction (or increase) in welfare enrollment.
- The number of passing grades on civic responsibility tests.
- The number of visits per student to libraries and museums.
- Students' attitudes toward themselves and others (as it is expected that the school environment will be kinder, more courteous interaction is anticipated throughout the school community).
- The percentage of the student population who regret the passing of the school year.
- The number of acts of vandalism.
- The number of graduates who are employed, pay taxes, and are registered to vote.
- The attendance patterns of students and teachers.
- The number of students who assign high marks to their teachers and schools 20 years after graduation.

These indicators underscore the importance of follow-up studies. As one teacher remarked, "If we carefully conduct longitudinal studies, we can be certain that our students will tell us how well we are doing." Boyer (1983, p. 135) confirms the importance of following up on graduates to learn what they do with their lives, successfully or not. This idea can be taken yet another step by suggesting that follow-up studies provide opportunities for students to evaluate their alma maters.

In regard to the second question raised by the educators — "Since many of these indicators are likely to be highly subjective, what should educators do to gain business community support for their use?" — there is no question that collecting data related to the suggested indicators would be difficult and expensive, but the information would provide a more valid indication of school performance than do existing methods. Certainly corporate leaders would need to be involved with teachers, parents, and students in developing such an assessment program. As one teacher noted: "Chief executive officers must buy into the agenda. The schools should increase their efforts to invite leaders of the business community to spend more time in the schools. Educators need to do more to make possible a 'marriage of and with our critics.'"

Perhaps more important than the acceptance of employers is the question of whether or not colleges and universities would accept reports containing alternative assessments when they are considering admission of students. Admissions officers may have difficulty selecting applicants under an alternative assessment system. Clearly, it is easier for them to make comparisons of Scholastic Aptitude Test scores and grade point averages.

A bank president who participated in the discussion at the retreat emphasized that he needed "students who can read, speak, and spell correctly, who have aspirations, and who are interested in moving ahead." It was suggested that he might require applicants to submit their school-work portfolios with their diplomas to provide a fuller idea of their abilities.

Many of the suggested alternative indicators are consistent with the explicit requirements of corporate leaders. But employers have a responsibility to help students understand their own responsibilities should they be hired; that is, students must be aware of what they need to know in order to succeed in the labor force. Alternative approaches to assessment would create practical as well as legal problems, since hiring decisions based on them would be largely subjective.

The business community must clearly identify and define the skills essential to employment and involve itself in the development of high school assessment mechanisms. The development of basic skills, problem-solving skills, positive attitudes toward work, the ability to work compatibly with others, and a sense of civic responsibility should be undertaken by family, school, and community.

Finally, the answer to the participants' third question — "Can performance-based or authentic approaches to assessment be used effectively as part of a national assessment program focusing on national standards?" — is, essentially, yes. The question, however, may overlook a key element of the issue, namely, that the most relevant goals are those developed at the level of the individual school with the involvement of the local community. Such goals encompass the diversity of local needs.

Alternative approaches to assessment will inevitably bring with them a number of difficulties. Development costs will be high. Additional time and funding will be required to administer and score the new assessments. Since these approaches are more subjective than current procedures, we should be open to the likelihood of a certain diminution of reliability in exchange for the increase in validity of educational assessment.

Among the key relationships and conflicts needing clarification and resolution are the results of individual student assessments, the national accountability movement, concerns regarding equity, the effects of new assessment approaches on students whose first language is not English, the alignment of new approaches with the curriculum, and the potential contribution of alternative assessments to teaching strategies.

The manner in which we assess school processes will play a key role in educating/preparing our best graduates of the future. New work undertaken in the area of cognition makes it clear that teaching and the assessment of student progress can be structured in a way that will better prepare students for the complex thinking required by contemporary life. Current political trends make it unlikely that the importance of testing will diminish. It is especially important, therefore, that we reformulate the assessment processes used in American education in ways that will tell us if we have effectively and appropriately prepared students to meet their own needs and those of society. Approaches to assessment based on performance can improve teaching strategies. At times it may be difficult to determine whether a given educational activity is part of the instructional program or part of a procedure to assess students' knowledge and understanding. Imagine this: The results of assessment efforts in the service of the instructional program!

BUSINESS AND UNIVERSITY COLLABORATION WITH THE SCHOOLS **11**

*Lewis C. Solmon and
Cheryl L. Fagnano*

The widespread perception that K-12 education in the United States has become less effective in recent decades than it was in the past has led many noneducational institutions to consider how they might help reverse this trend, particularly through various types of collaboration. Although some of the planning for collaboration may be initiated for altruistic reasons (to produce better educated citizens, for example, who make a stronger democracy, or to ensure more equal opportunity), the self-interest of the collaborators is a strong motive as well.

Both sides feel the effects of inadequately prepared graduates. In particular, the corporate sector sees the quality of the available labor force declining, as evidenced by the low reading, writing, mathematical, and critical thinking skills of job applicants and job holders. Similarly, universities are compelled to compensate for the poor preparation of incoming freshmen by devoting increasing resources to remedial courses and to programs that should have been offered in high school.

A number of indicators contribute to a sense among businesses and universities that their human, financial, and intellectual resources could significantly help in the educational arena. These include the eroding of the resource base in K-12 education, the questionable competence of some K-12 staff, and the impossible demands placed on teachers who are increasingly doing duty as surrogate parents, spiritual advisers, and counselors. As schools recognize these same problems, they have begun to look beyond their traditional sources of support for the resources that will allow them to do their best.

The environment is not only ripe for collaboration, it has already spawned a very large number of education-business partnerships. The National Center for Educational Statistics (1989) reports that between 1983-84 and 1987-88 the number of business-school partnerships nationwide rose from 42,200 to 140,800. And in a 1990 *Fortune* magazine survey of Fortune 500 and Service 500 companies, all but 2 percent of the 305 businesses responding were involved in some kind of K-12 educational efforts (see McManus, 1990). These programs addressed a range of issues,

from drug abuse and dropout prevention to career awareness and character education, with academic subjects in between. These partnerships were diverse in other
ways as well: They involved large and small businesses; took place in urban, suburban, and rural settings; and included more than 9 million students (Business
Roundtable, 1989; National Center for Educational Statistics, 1989).

During the Milken Family Foundation National Educator Awards Retreat, the
award recipients — all exemplary practitioners — discussed educational collaborations. Whether between schools and businesses or schools and universities, the
collaborations were examined, first, in the context of impediments to their success
and, second, in terms of successful examples. Throughout this discussion we will
cite both survey data and specific collaborations that highlight either the impediments or the conditions that promote success that have been identified.

A key impediment to school-business partnerships attaches to the attitudes on
both sides. A presumption on the part of businesspeople that their expertise exceeds
that of teachers can engender considerable resentment among educators. It can even
lead them to resist assistance. Schools, for their part, may also resist partnerships
if they think such collaboration makes them appear to be troubled.

The different institutional cultures of schools, universities, and corporations
may also make interaction difficult. Reward structures, which are fundamental to
the success of any program, vary significantly across institutions. Also, schools
often do not know whom to approach in a corporation or university. Similarly,
those outside the school may be uncertain whether to offer their help at the level of
the district, the school, or even the classroom teacher.

Business leaders can become involved in short-term, high-profile programs that
have little educational substance. Cooperative programs should be based on more
than a general desire to be helpful or visible. Too often, partners fail to set goals and
establish evaluation criteria, making it difficult to determine whether or not efforts
have been successful. And when programs are terminated, schools rarely have the
resources to continue them on their own.

The fact that it is easier to recommend programs than to pay for them is another pitfall. Many educators believe that businesses often prefer to give advice or to
get involved in gimmicky projects rather than make substantial investments of time,
money, or both. A self-promoting program is more likely to be supported than a real
solution that costs money. A corporate CEO taking a few hours off to teach in a
ghetto classroom during "partnership week" may provide good press for his firm,
but probably does not help children at the school. The same CEO may be quite
reluctant to allow employees to take time off on a regular basis to visit their children's schools, despite the reported benefits of parental participation on student
achievement (Oakes & Lipton, 1990). Many firms fear the resultant disruption
will be counterproductive and costly.

Despite these impediments, collaborative efforts *are* increasing, and many of
them are thought to be highly productive. Following are retreat participants'
views on what constitutes a successful collaboration. The discussion focuses on

four key characteristics: Collaborations should be mutually beneficial; they should make use of the expertise of collaborators; they should involve those with solid influence; and they should focus on what is possible. Successful collaborations must involve mutual benefits. *Mutual benefits*, in this context, denotes two things: (a) that each partner receive desired outcomes, and (b) that the giving flows in two directions. Successful collaboration between K-12 schools and other institutions include the recognition that, though the rewards for each side may be different, they must exist.

The coincidence of the heightened potential for and the escalated rhetoric of university-school collaborations suggests the need to look closely at the mutual benefits of such partnerships. Over the long term, universities will benefit from better-trained incoming freshmen who will need less remedial-level instruction. Public institutions have an additional incentive to collaborate, as they are funded by state legislatures that might conceivably punish universities with lower budget allocations if K-12 education continues to lag. Hence, the intensified rhetoric of university leaders urging their faculty to increase their involvement with K-12 education.

Put differently, business needs a well-educated work force that will not require expensive remedial training before becoming productive. Universities and colleges need well-prepared entering freshmen. Schools need serious opportunities to help keep kids in school longer and to develop effective curricula for all types of students. Programs that work toward all of these goals will have the best chance of long-term success.

Work-service programs for students that call on teachers for program development, implementation, and assessment are good examples of mutual-benefit programs. In such programs, students can earn money and gain experience in the work world while accumulating school credit. And schools may lower dropout rates while giving trial runs to innovative curricula. The corporations, for their part, receive relatively inexpensive labor and the opportunity to "preview" potential full-time employees. In fact, 76 percent of corporations responding to the *Fortune* survey cited above had offered students summer or part-time jobs.

Material and equipment donations to schools by corporations can be mutually beneficial. Schools get materials they otherwise might not have, and corporations get tax write-offs. Indeed, the *Fortune* survey indicates that 64 percent of the companies responding contributed materials or equipment to schools. However, practitioners stress that it is important that materials donated be given in complete and usable form. Retreat participants pointed out that the beneficial effects of such donations can be sharply undercut unless funds are provided for necessary teacher training when items such as computers are donated.

Another mutually beneficial arrangement is for business to offer teachers summer employment, as 26 percent of the *Fortune* survey respondents did. Such employment may supplement low salaries enough to allow talented educators to remain in a profession they might otherwise have to abandon. It can also have an invigorating effect on educators' teaching. The benefits to corporations of such employment are clear: They gain a talented new employment pool from which to draw. The effects of such collaborations on the corporate bottom line, however, and on the improvement of a permanent labor force are for now less clear.

The impact on a business firm of giving employees time to tutor or teach in the schools are also thus far unclear. The benefits to schools, however, are quite clear. Of corporations responding to the *Fortune* survey, 50 percent said they encouraged employees to teach or tutor, and 12 percent said they loaned their executives to schools. These arrangements can provide strong supplements for overburdened school staffs, especially when they provide teaching help in such understaffed areas as mathematics.

An example of this type of program was started in South Central Los Angeles several years ago by Michael Milken. Mike's Math Club is dedicated to raising the level of interest and proficiency in mathematics among elementary school students. Currently, more than 2,000 fifth- and sixth-grade students participate in regular programing conducted in both Spanish and English by volunteers.

The initiatives discussed thus far fit in the first three categories of business-school collaborations identified by P. Michael Timpane and Laurie Miller McNeill (1991) in a study titled *Business Impact on Education and Child Development Reform*. According to their topology, the first stage of involvement is a "Helping Hand" partnership, in which business provides goods and services, followed by "Programmatic Initiatives," and "Compacts and Collaborative Efforts," which attempt school reform through program initiatives.

The last stage of involvement is said to be one in which business leaders and organizations become directly involved in policy and reform at various levels of education and government. Initiatives in this so-called final stage of cooperation between business and schools are popular and plentiful. For example, significant numbers of the *Fortune* survey respondents encourage employees to run for school boards (59 percent), lobby legislatures for reform (22 percent), and actively support education-related tax increases or bond issues (18 percent). These forms of assistance proffered by companies to public schools are, however, less direct, less expensive, and less likely to be effective than direct sustained financial and material support to local schools. Thus, some have taken issue with Timpane and McNeill's characterization of their stages of school-business relationships as "sequential ... and progressively more significant to educational reform and improvement." For example, current lobbying efforts by corporations on behalf of schools have not been very effective, as evidenced by the failure of most recent efforts to get more government or public funds directed to the schools.

Universities and schools can also develop mutually beneficial collaborations. In fact, universities may be better equipped than corporations to help K-12 education. Although universities are not likely to provide direct financial help, they possess other useful expertise and resources.

First, university faculty members have access to the latest developments in their fields, which they can pass on to K-12 teachers. The American Association of Higher Education has reported on school-university collaborations in its periodical, *Current Issues in Higher Education*; see in particular a recent article by Gaudiani and Burnett (1985/86) titled "Academic Alliances: A New Approach to School/College Collaboration." Academic alliances are programs in which university and K-12 faculty work together on the teaching and learning of academic disciplines. The focus is on the various disciplines, as they are considered the broadest common ground between school and college faculty (Gaudiani & Burnett, 1985/86). Alliances for foreign languages, history, international studies, geography, English, science, and mathematics have been created across the United States, and thousands of college and school faculty members have been involved.

Further, schools of education and psychology programs should be able to inform K-12 educators in the latest ideas and research in the development and learning processes of children as well as on how best to teach. Education schools also train new professionals for the schools. Management schools could also offer advice, not only on management, but on business and the organizational challenges of K-12 education.

Over the last 25 years, educational research has proceeded at an unprecedented rate. While there is still much to be learned about modes of teaching, learning, and evaluation, there has been considerable research progress in these areas, and a great deal of the research has been published. The dissemination of such material to practitioners, however, is not rewarded by research universities. As long as such universities emphasize and reward research and scholarly productivity while paying scant attention to community service or professional involvement, faculty interest in school collaborations is likely to remain faint.

As the system now operates, schools have little incentive to allow researchers into the classroom. Outside research can disrupt regular classroom activity, and the educational hierarchy, as it stands, tends to rank the classroom teacher below the university professor.

One potentially effective form of collaboration, particularly with education school faculty, is the use of elementary and secondary schools as de facto research laboratories. An important element of such a plan would be an agreement on the part of the university partner to disseminate results of previous successful studies to school practitioners, who would benefit by improvements in such areas as pedagogy and curriculum development. And to the extent that a by-product of collaboration is research papers, in the publish-or-perish world of academe, faculty would have the needed incentive to get involved with the schools. These activities and the good public relations that accrue to the cooperating universities may provide the short-term benefits necessary to stimulate increased cooperation between schools and universities.

It is crucial in school-business partnerships that collaborators contribute their own expertise as they work toward program goals. A sure path to failure is for one member of the team to assume the role or the responsibility of another.

Collaborative projects work best when all participants clearly identify their own potential contributions and their expectations of the others. A corporate CEO may know little about improving the literacy skills of high school graduates but a good deal about problem solving and motivation. Teachers and school administrators, on the other hand, may know little about the human resource needs of a corporation but a great deal about how to teach reading. In such a case, both have a strong incentive for developing a collaborative literacy project or enhancing the basic skills curriculum in local schools. When both sides offer their native talents and accept those of their partners, educational problems and work force problems may be solved positively and creatively.

Of the 48 percent of corporations responding to the *Fortune* survey who indicated they participated in school partnerships, it remains unclear what the exact nature of the participation was. Whether it included some of the activities cited above or whether it involved firms' providing advice on school operations, the survey does not specify. What must be determined, however, is whether or not schools are receiving expert assistance. There is some irony in corporations offering management "expertise" to schools even as they seek new keys to deal with their own declining productivity and increasing international competition.

The key players in a collaborative effort must have the ability to make decisions and to commit resources to seeing the project through. Influence — or clout — is not defined by the absolute extent of one's resources or authority, but rather by the extent to which participants have the ability to get the job done. Indeed, it is possible to envision a very successful collaboration between a single classroom teacher and a retired worker seeking to share skills learned over a lifetime in their respective work worlds. Their resources and authority may amount to only their personal time and energy, but this sort of collaboration can prove as successful as any developed between a CEO and a superintendent.

Any successful collaboration must focus on the possible. To begin with, when defining the problem it is probably best to think small. It is unwise to try to solve a problem greater than one has the resources to handle. The dropout problem in this country, for example, is enormous, and individual schools and businesses likely do not have the resources to address this issue concretely. However, we know that poor school attendance and low academic achievement are antecedents to dropping out of school, and we know that increased parental involvement in school has been reported to have a positive effect on attendance and achievement (Oakes & Lipton, 1990). Perhaps a local school-business partnership could devise a creative method for increasing parental involvement, something as simple as installing telephones in classrooms to facilitate parent-teacher communication, for instance. This minor change could have a significant impact on parental involvement and school enrollment.

Another aspect of the importance of focusing on what is possible concerns realistic thinking about resources. A school seeking support for a dropout prevention program, for example, should make sure that the program is well defined and within the realm of possibility given the resources of the institutions being considered for assistance. In the same manner, schools must evaluate their ability to bend with the demands of a collaborative effort. A corporate sponsor looking for a school partner for a work-study program may want to define the program in such a way that it will connect students' work experience with an aspect of the school curriculum.

A final thought on the subject of what is possible. It is incorrect to assume that unless there are vast supplies of money and other resources available a program cannot be successfully undertaken. Business and educational leaders — whether from small towns, rural areas, or large urban centers — should not wait until they are ready to solve the problems of education before they begin to develop cooperative plans for educational improvement. Concerned participants should begin immediately, with whatever resources are available. Rural areas, for instance, often lack major corporate or private funding sources to be tapped, but they can nonetheless develop significant and successful programs by drawing on local resources. Small-town businesses are sometimes in a better position to motivate their employees to participate in projects in which they have personal interest than are large corporations that are merely exercising their civic duty.

Parents, of course, are another important source of support and participation for collaborative projects. They can often deploy their professional experiences, whether in the classroom as instructors or as liaisons to their employers. Retired people, members of the military, and other volunteers are also promising, untapped resources for programs, especially in small towns.

The National Educator Award recipients identified a number of exemplary collaborative efforts working in every corner of the country. TRW, a California-based aerospace corporation, gives schools computers and provides computer training programs for teachers. Illinois Bell in Chicago has provided 26 schools with grants of $10,000 to develop innovative educational ideas. IBM and Apple Computer support programs that place computers in classrooms as well as programs designed to ensure that the equipment is integrated into the regular curriculum.

The Scripps Institute and local schools in La Jolla, California, have programs in which students learn about environmental issues. Firms such as State Farm Insurance and Morgan Stanley & Co. have developed programs providing jobs and training for students while they are in school. The Kroeger Stores in Cincinnati, Ohio, have developed an innovative program intended to provide college funds for low-income students: Beginning as early as the elementary level, students with superior academic and attendance records can earn up to $300 per quarter toward college. Such incentives are critical for students who otherwise may never have contemplated college.

Numerous university-sponsored programs have been developed to provide in-service teacher training programs. UCLA's Center for Academic Interinstitutional Programs, for example, provides summer stipends that allow teachers to attend courses to expand their particular areas of interest or knowledge of their academic field. The Cal-Arts Project allows university faculty to work with K-12 teachers on arts programs.

To review, for either corporations or universities to be a real help to our K-12 schools, several steps must be taken:

1. Collaborators with the schools must realize that the ultimate rewards will be evident only over the long term, probably measurable in generations.
2. In the meantime, there are short-term benefits, such as improved public relations, inexpensive labor for firms, or research sites for faculty members. If the schools want other sectors to participate in improving education, they must recognize these short-term needs and help achieve them.
3. Short-term assessment mechanisms must be established.
4. There must be real commitment and leadership at the highest levels of all partners. Corporate CEOs must be willing to commit real money (not just obsolete equipment that can serve as a tax write-off), and they should be flexible about freeing employees to perform various tasks in schools. They may have to sacrifice a small percentage of the short-term bottom line in order to improve profits (and society) in the longer run. University leaders must work to improve the incentive system for faculty rewards if they expect to see school-university collaborations.

Finally, it is small, identifiable changes that should be expected from collaborative efforts, rather than a sea of change in educational efficacy. In a 1984 paper titled "Small Wins," psychologist Karl E. Weick suggested that on many fronts much can be accomplished through small steps instead of waiting for the ideal solution. According to Weick:

> People often define social problems in ways that overwhelm their ability to do anything about them … When the magnitude of problems is scaled upward in the interest of mobilizing action, the quality of thought and action declines, because processes such as frustration, arousal, and helplessness are activated … To recast larger problems into smaller, less arousing problems, people can identify a series of controllable opportunities of modest size that produce visible results (p. 40).

Lately, corporate and university leaders seem to have been swept up in the panic over the state of our nation's schools, and are breathlessly trying to find solutions in such long term efforts as voucher systems or the establishment of schools run by corporations for the state. Many of todays best educators would suggest that the wisest course is to to take small steps in the interim and find gratification — and results — in small wins.

Lewis C. Solmon

Program planners and representatives of the National Educator Award winners agreed that whatever the type of graduates we ultimately may want, certain processes must be undertaken if we are to achieve our goals. Teachers have to work with parents and other community institutions, for example, to instill appropriate values and attitudes in students; steps have to be taken toward meeting the needs of diverse student populations; high-quality teachers have to be attracted and trained; changes in the organization and structure of schools have to be made; school effectiveness has to be accurately assessed; and other sectors, particularly universities and businesses, have to become involved in K-12 education. Though this list may not be an exhaustive description of what is needed in the effort to achieve truly successful public schools for our nation, we believe most would agree that the processes cited here are crucial to the enterprise.

The very large number of elements in school reform is more than equaled by the number of different views on how most effectively and efficiently to meet the goals of the six areas focused on here. Each of the preceding six chapters describes the discussion of an area addressed, and each provides valuable insights offered by some of the top practitioners in the country. What follows in this chapter derives in part from the summary statements presented at the retreat and includes thoughts of my own that not only refer to the broad literature, but that have also benefitted from time for reflection, the absence of group dynamics, and, most particularly, the views put forth at the retreat. Although the ideas expressed here are not necessarily subscribed to by retreat participants, some of what follows actually underscores what has preceded it.

VALUES

Since we all agree that students should leave school with more than just the ability to count, spell, and recite facts, it seems hard to disagree with the need for our schools to instill appropriate values and attitudes in youngsters. A problem arises early, however, when we attempt even a definition of *appropriate*. Former Secretary of Education Lauro Cavazos (1990) finds it puzzling that the question so often arises as to which values — or whose — are to be taught. To raise the question at all implies that as a nation we have no values in common — that there is, indeed, nothing worth instilling in every schoolchild. That is not true — or, at the very least, it *should not* be true.

California State Superintendent of Instruction Bill Honig (1990) wonders why many people are uncomfortable with the idea of public schools' instructing children on matters of ethics and morals. As he points out, children are not born with these traits. One could hardly oppose the goal of graduating students who are moral and ethical, but these terms are subject to many interpretations. Thomas Lickona (1988a) has said that citizens in a democracy must both understand and be committed to upholding the morals that underpin it — respect for law and the rights of individuals, for instance, voluntary participation in public life, concern for the common good. Lickona goes on to say that communities are discovering that, pluralism notwithstanding, common moral ground based on respect and responsibility *can* be found.

Even were we all to agree on the need for a common set of values, there is still the fear of projecting "white, middle-class values" on students who are neither white nor middle-class. This is a projection that leads to so-called value-neutral education, the clear assumption of which is that there are no values common to all Americans — whatever their race, ethnic heritage, or socioeconomic status. In my view, educators have (a) not spent enough time either identifying universal values appropriate for all children or figuring the best ways to present those values, and (b) spent too much time ensuring that no one be offended by the instilling of another's values.

As the contents of our melting pot combined to make a rich stew, we should spend less time fretting about the mix of ingredients and more time nourishing the most people possible. Any value system propagated by our public schools must acknowledge *both* the particular strengths of the individuals and groups that comprise our society and the similarities among groups that allow us to be a single nation. With the breaking up of the Soviet Union, the term *balkanization* has become especially evocative. One need consider only briefly the plight of Ireland, of Yugoslavia, of Lebanon, to see how ravaged a country can be by internal differences. It is imperative that we recognize the causes of unrest in so many other nations before we support an extreme model of separatism in this country. If we do not hold common values, we do not have a nation, and an essential social mission of our schools surely must be the maintaining of a national identity.

The increase in the ethnic mix in many parts of the United States, coupled with decreased responsibility on the part of the family, religious organizations, and community groups, makes the transmission of values more difficult even as it shifts the burden onto schools already strapped for time. A convergence of pressures is squeezing schools: The pool of knowledge has expanded, more voices than ever are demanding a hearing *within* the curriculum, employers are demanding a ready-to-work work force, and schools are expected to offer an array of extra-academic topics ranging from health education to driver's education. The result: The time left for traditional academic instruction — to say nothing of increased instruction in values and ethics — is ever more compressed. One question demanding an answer is: Which responsibilities of the school must be sacrificed in order to free up time for the inculcation of values? Put differently, is it, in fact, possible to conduct values education as part of the regular academic curriculum? Progress *can* be made in the integration of values by means of the choices of civilizations studied, literature read, and concepts promulgated. By means of what is taught, how it is taught, and how the learning of it is evaluated and rewarded, we can demonstrate a set of appropriate values.

In my view, virtually all of the values expressed in this report represent noble goals. In what follows, I would like to highlight a few that were themes of the retreat and to add to them.

Bill Honig (1990) advocates helping students to develop a sense of purpose, to feel a part of a nurturing community, and to believe in themselves enough to resist peer pressure. In essence, Honig says that children must take control of their lives and perceive the ethical choices inherent in daily activities. Instructional programs should give youngsters experience in decision making, in developing tolerance, in understanding democracy, and in grasping our ethical culture. These, I believe, are sensible goals.

Something one hears too little about these days is the value of hard work, of persistence, of earning — not expecting — success, of taking responsibility for one's own destiny. As an economist, I consistently encourage teaching cost-benefit analysis and the concept of opportunity costs. The idea that achieving one benefit means incurring some kind of cost and the idea that, in an environment of limited resources, having one thing means not having another are essential concepts for guiding choices and determining behavior. These ideas are what inform the understanding that there are consequences to one's behavior; that sometimes the cost of an action — whether to another or to oneself — may far outweigh the benefits. Taking the long view rather than seeking instant gratification is another economic concept that has much application to our context, and it, too, is often omitted from the list of values we hope our children will derive from their school experience. Finally, we must remember that life is reciprocal. Each of us has a responsibility to contribute to our family, our school, our community, and our world.

Though there may seem a contradiction in advocating enlisting parents and community organizations to inculcate values when, in fact, it is the abdication of so many parents and groups that has shifted the task onto the schools, I believe that from the perspective of the educator, the involvement of parents (or anyone else, for that matter) in values education can only be a plus. That said, the ultimate responsibility for what goes on in our schools falls, as ever, to the teacher.

Thomas Lickona (1988a) has suggested a number of ways that teachers can help provide moral education in the classroom:

1. Serve as moral models and mentors for children.
2. Develop a cohesive classroom community in which students know each other, care about each other, and feel a part of the group.
3. Have children strive for a high standard of academic responsibility so that they may understand the value of work in a way that develops their character and moves them to contribute to the human community.
4. Handle discipline in a way that develops the moral reasoning of children and encourages them to discipline themselves, to comply voluntarily with rules.
5. Provide opportunities for group decision making and shared responsibility.
6. Teach skills of cooperation.
7. Develop students' capacity for moral reflection through discussion and debate on moral issues drawn from basic subject areas.
8. Use inspiring role models from history and current events.

I agree with the educators who participated in the retreat that values education and the instilling of ethics in our students are important and noble goals. I would urge that we identify a broad set of values that apply to youngsters in virtually any classroom in the country regardless of its hetero- or homogeneity. Tolerance of differences is surely a central value that we must aim for. It is not, however, the only one. Some might well eschew the need to strive for traditional success as defined here. I am reluctant to exclude from any list of values and attitudes, however, the characteristics that have led to success as defined up to the present in this country. But this is yet another value judgment, and perhaps we must emphasize to our children that they have the right to reject received wisdom.

DIVERSITY

Any discussion of this kind leads naturally into consideration of the issues surrounding diversity. It must be agreed that every student should graduate from our nation's public schools with an understanding of and tolerance for people who are different from him or her. That is, it must be recognized that everyone — whatever his or her background — has an identical right to achieve.

I appreciate that debate at the retreat took diversity to include not only differences in race, ethnic origin, and culture, but also religion, physical disability, sexual preference, and economic status. All too often the term *diversity* is construed as applying to race alone, and yet the problems of educational achievement and economic success are far more likely to involve differences in family income than differences in race. As William J. Wilson argues in his 1987 study *The Truly*

Disadvantaged, the factors associated with the worsening plight of low-income blacks are exceedingly complex and extend beyond the issue of contemporary discrimination. Indeed, it is not unreasonable to say that race-specific policies stemming from the civil rights movement, although beneficial to more advantaged blacks (that is, those with higher incomes, more education, and more prestigious jobs), do little for the truly disadvantaged. The essential point is not that the worsening conditions of the ghetto underclass are a function of the improved conditions of other blacks who have benefitted from race-specific programs; the point is, rather, that these programs are mistaken for appropriate solutions to the problems of *all* blacks, regardless of economic class.

Harold Hodgkinson (1989e) has pointed out the spectacular (radical) changes in the nature of today's student population. The fact is that at least one-third of the nation's children are at risk of failure in school even before they enter kindergarten. Since 1987, one-fourth of all preschool children in the United States have been living in poverty. In addition, about 350,000 children per year are born to mothers addicted to cocaine during pregnancy. Approximately 15 million children are being reared by single mothers whose annual family incomes average approximately $11,400 (in 1988 dollars) — which is within $1,000 of the poverty line. Some 20 percent of America's preschool children have not been vaccinated against polio. Only 6 percent of U.S. households today include a working father, a housewife mother, and two children of school age. One-fourth of pregnant mothers receive no physical care of any sort during the crucial first trimester of pregnancy. About 20 percent of handicapped children would not be impaired had their mothers had one physical exam during the first trimester. According to the Children's Defense Fund, (1991) at least 2 million children have no adult supervision after school. On any night, it is estimated that between 68,000 and 500,000 children have no homes in which to sleep, and while there is disagreement over the number of homeless children, all agree the number in growing. And a total of 2.4 million children were reported abused or neglected in 1989, a 147 percent increase since 1979.

In sum, roughly one-third of preschool children are destined for school failure because of poverty, neglect, sickness, handicapping conditions, and lack of adult protection and nurturance. Such children come from every racial and ethnic group. It is clear that even to begin to repair this problem and to provide equal opportunities for students from diverse backgrounds will require the efforts of many people and organizations — health and social welfare agencies, parents, and business and political leaders (Hodgkinson, 1989e).

Thus, providing equal educational opportunity implies much more than providing a multicultural awareness for students. Tolerance and indeed celebration of individual and group differences are important. The needs of individual students must be assessed and met. Prejudging individuals as members of particular groups whose average needs and potential are thought to be at a certain level accomplishes little if anything. Only after these goals are achieved can we begin to find and strive for "equal educational opportunity."

Equal educational opportunity is more easily accepted as an abstract objective than as a universally accepted definition. Clearly, the term does not refer simply to access to an educational institution. In recent decades many legislative and judicial initiatives have attempted to ensure that all students have access to equivalent resources in their schools. If students enter school with differing motivations, preparation, abilities, and support, however, providing access to equal resources at school will not result in equal educational achievement or equal outcomes. Depending upon one's definition of *equal educational opportunity*, the fact that all students do not demonstrate equal achievement by the time they leave school does not necessarily imply that the educational experiences per se were unequal. Unless we are willing to identify individual differences, particularly among students in the same racial and ethnic groups, we will never be able to provide the resources required to achieve equal educational outcomes.

Diversity in the schools is usually discussed in one of two contexts. The first sees a need to ensure that individuals who start the process at a disadvantage are given the help necessary to achieve their highest potential. The other sees the need to offer students from diverse backgrounds an education that recognizes the contributions to our nation's and the world's knowledge and culture by members of groups other than white males from the middle class.

The first context includes compensatory or remedial education. I would like to expand the concept to include a concern that all students — including those at the top of the ability, income, and support distribution — achieve their maximum potential. In recent years, I have frequently observed the shifting of funds in the public schools from gifted and honors programs to remedial and compensatory programs. Our nation may be doing as much of a disservice to our very best students by failing to nurture them as we are doing to those more difficult-to-educate students when we ignore them. From an economic growth perspective, we might ask the following key — and as yet unanswered — question: Is our international competitive edge hurt more by known low achievers reading at a sixth-grade level when they should be at an eighth-grade level, or by a consistent failure to identify and encourage the brightest 5 percent? The best solution, would be to pursue both of these goals — namely, remediation at the bottom and full development at the top. Resource constraints, however, generally preclude our pursuing both goals at the same time. This is a decision — economic, social, and moral — that society must make.

The second area of concern over diversity sets a goal of developing a multicultural sensitivity in teachers, administrators, and students, and providing textbooks and curricula that reflect not only our Western tradition (that is, democracy, tolerance of differences, freedom of speech and religion, and respect for the law) but also the contributions to that tradition made by those tracing their heritages to Asia, Africa, and Central and South America. While there may be some merit to this goal, it is simplistic to think that such an equation will necessarily ensure higher achievement among minority and culturally diverse students. With limited time and inadequate resources for teaching materials such as up-to-date textbooks, schools will be constantly obliged to decide what should be eliminated from the curriculum to free up time for more culturally diverse components. This takes us back to the issue of values and to whether each constituency in a culturally diverse school system has a right to confine itself primarily to culturally congruent ideas, or whether all students should be exposed to a common core of knowledge.

The question arises, for example: Can there ever be a "bias-free" textbook, or are we merely substituting one bias for another? Are the conclusions drawn by students who have been free to think creatively and critically in school as valid as any other conclusions? From some quarters (most particularly from some of our leading institutions of higher education) we hear voiced the view that any one perspective is as valid as the next — that is, that there is no right answer to an analytical question. Is *this* the direction we want our schools to take?

All would agree that the unjust or harmful treatment of children from diverse cultures cannot be tolerated. Yet even an axiom as basic as this becomes complicated by the effort to define *harmful*. If a student from one culture does not smile when walking past a student from another, is that *harmful*? There must be norms of acceptable behavior having to do with respect, emotional security, and the appreciation of diversity. Does that mean, however, that study of *The Merchant of Venice* should be banned because of its depiction of Jews? Does appreciating differences necessarily imply that negative references and images must be ignored?

We must confront diversity with sensitivity. We must define equal educational opportunity and then strive to provide it. It is important to recognize, however, that many goals that have noble veneers are very complex below the surface. Some of our most widely accepted aims, in fact, are fraught with value judgments. And attached to many of the benefits we seek in such domains as sensitivity, cultural awareness, and equal opportunity may be costs as well.

QUALITY TEACHERS

As the public schools' responsibilities expand with the addition of tasks and the broadening of constituencies, the challenges facing teachers increase proportionately. It is imperative that there be teachers in every classroom who are equal to these challenges. The media, public policymakers, educational reformers, and teachers unions, however, tell us that today's teacher recruits do not issue from the ranks of "the best and the brightest," that they are ill prepared, underpaid, and working under difficult and sometimes dangerous conditions, and that many of them leave the profession within five years.

How, then, are we to attract top-notch, well-trained professionals who are committed to remaining in the classroom and dedicated to staying abreast of developments in their field? Following is a response from an economist's perspective.

While I do not agree wholeheartedly with Broudy's (1980) suggestion that "the goal of putting an inspirational teacher in every classroom is one of the great mischievous illusions of our time," I do believe we must acknowledge certain realities as we seek to staff our classrooms in the coming years. These realities include the sheer number of teachers needed; the characteristics of the profession; the recruitment, training, and even retraining of teachers; and the cost-benefit relationships inherent in change.

To begin with, it is likely that at least 850,000 — a phenomenal number — new teachers will be needed in the United States within this decade to meet replacement and expansion demands. We cannot realistically expect to fill these openings from only our most talented groups. In 1980, for example, there were 186,000 college graduates judged to be in the upper quartile of achievement (Plisko, 1983, Table 4.2). Even if the typical 80 percent of this top quartile who seek jobs upon graduation had all gone into teaching, demand would have still exceeded supply by 30,000 (Lanier & Little, 1986). What we can and should do is ensure that all our classrooms are staffed by well-trained, capable professionals, some of whom will be exceptional, but all of whom will be competent.

Three general areas have been suggested as routes to assuring a supply of high-quality of teachers: compensation, status/working conditions, and training. In the best of all possible worlds, of course, the solution would be to provide higher compensation, increased status and improved working conditions, and better training for all teachers. We do not, alas, live in an uncomplicated world; we occupy a world of trade-offs and opportunity costs, a world of competing interests in which benefits have costs and the achievement of goals demands realism.

It is axiomatic that if teacher salaries were higher, then more people would enter and remain in the profession. The salary increases of the last couple of years have contributed to an increased interest in teaching. Nevertheless, there is simply not enough money available to hoist teachers' salaries to the average level of compensation accorded lawyers, MBAs, or medical doctors.

This said, it should be pointed out that the gap between teachers' salaries and those of other professions is not as great as is generally thought. First, a teacher's salary must be adjusted for a full working year. As teachers are engaged in their profession for 9 or 10 months a year, it is unrealistic that they be compensated at the rate of professionals working 12 months. Indeed, one of the key attractions of the the teaching profession is what Dan Lortie (1975) has termed "time compatibility." In essence, those who choose to teach often do so, if only in part, because the profession's time sequencing provides blocks of discretionary time. For this benefit, one must be willing or able to sacrifice income.

Teachers' salary schedules, furthermore, often understate actual earnings because they do not include the salary increments that can be had by taking on such extra tasks as coaching, supervising extracurricular activities, overload teaching, and summer work. We tend to think of salaries in terms of those earned by the most successful in the profession. Obviously, the best lawyers earn salaries many times greater than those of the best teachers. Lawyers working in various levels of government, however, or lawyers with small practices and lower-income clients do not have incomes all that much greater than teachers. The point is that the most successful lawyers earn substantially more than the least successful ones, whereas the best teachers (controlling for education and seniority) rarely make substantially more than those who are less effective.

Such reasoning argues for a teaching pay scale that accords better pay to the more successful. In essence, this is a merit pay plan in which the best — say, the top 25 percent of teachers — would earn substantially more than the rest. Though such plans are vigorously opposed by many educators, I believe that nearly all arguments against merit pay for teachers can be answered. Indeed, the conditions that are said to preclude a merit system in education exist in many other professions, including the law and medicine. The question is this: Would more of our better-qualified college graduates enter the teaching profession if salaries were based more on merit? The recent record suggests the answer is yes.

Before the women's movement, most women seeking careers had a choice of nursing or teaching, with virtually all women who couldn't stand the sight of blood opting to teach. Thus, a sizable proportion of our nation's best and brightest "better half" entered the teaching profession *faute de mieux*. Today, an unprecedented number of women are entering professions such as business, medicine, and law — professions that reward merit and individual effort. Although teaching by nature retains its appeal for some very bright and capable women, for the most part women (and men) choose careers that will reward their own accomplishments, and so they have selected careers other than teaching.

Since most observers agree that is is virtually impossible to rectify the differences in salaries between typical teachers and typical professionals in other fields, the importance of salary tends to be minimized. Some surveys indicate that teachers feel other aspects of teaching are more important than salary with regard to job satisfaction (Lortie, 1975). Such responses may, however, reflect the fact that teachers have pretty much given up on the salary issue, and that they seek satisfaction in other areas. Alternatively, they may confirm that those who go into the teaching profession are not interested in making a great deal of money. These responses tell us nothing, of course, about the possibility of another sort of person entering the profession were salaries higher in general, or even higher for the very best.

If the issue of salary is not important in the beginning of a teacher's career, it certainly becomes so once he or she has a family and contemplates buying a house. This is a significant factor in why so many teachers remain in the profession for fewer than five years. Parenthetically, if we concede the inevitability of a salary ceiling for teachers, we may have to adjust to the idea of teaching being a short-term career. Some have suggested a "Peace Corps model" for teaching, in which significant numbers of college graduates would spend up to five years in teaching before moving on to other careers. Were there a steady stream of replacements, such a model might allow us to maintain a higher-quality teacher work force than currently exists.

How can teachers acquire greater status? We must first recognize that status is a relative concept. I have long argued that when teachers are able to live as well as lawyers, the status of the two professions will equilibrate. According to Dan Lortie, the teaching profession has traditionally been an important route into the middle class, particularly for men from low socioeconomic backgrounds. This trend has changed little since Lortie's 1975 study.

According to a 1987 report, *New Teachers in the Job Market*, almost 50 percent of newly qualified teachers come from families in which neither parent attended college (Frankel & Stowe, 1987). In fact, the average teacher salary of $28,000 is within a few hundred dollars of the average or "middle class" salary for all full-time workers in the United States (U.S. Bureau of the Census, 1990). Average teachers' salaries, however, are not usually compared with other average salaries, but with salaries in higher-paid professions, most of which require similar levels of education. Middle-class status is construed as the ability to buy a home, to send one's children to the college of their choice, and to provide for a comfortable retirement — all things difficult to do in 1991 on $28,000 a year. From the perspective of an immigrant or a poor minority family, however, $28,000 may indeed be a significant socioeconomic improvement.

This is not to imply that minorities and low-income students should be confined to the teaching profession alone, or that we can pay teachers less because for many whatever they make is already an economic improvement. Rather, it is a recognition of a congruence of interests of society in general, and the emerging black middle class in particular, and a recognition of several key aspects of the teaching profession. First, teaching is a relatively uncomplicated field to enter, and people can take it up at many points in their lives. State colleges and teacher training institutions, for example, are affordable and do not have elitist admission standards. Moreover, owing to the important concern over educating the increasing number of minority and culturally diverse students, men and women from these backgrounds are being offered unprecedented opportunities for entering the profession. Finally, teaching provides more job security than do most professions without tenure. For one used to a market where jobs are hard to find and/or hold, these features could be quite appealing.

An improvement in teachers' relative status is not all that matters, however; an improvement in their absolute status is important as well. In addition to financial remuneration, issues of training and of professionalism tend to pose problems in the context of increasing the absolute level of teachers' status. Regarding professionalism, it has been frequently argued in recent years that were teachers given a more active role in running the schools and had they more authority over both educational and managerial matters, the prestige of the job of teaching would increase accordingly. This issue overlaps with that of restructuring, which will be discussed below. An obvious question arising in the meantime, however, is: Do teachers as currently trained have the skills required of managers? It is worth repeating that taking teachers out of the classroom to perform management tasks incurs additional costs and likely certain trade-offs. Giving teachers a certain percentage of the workday off in order to plan or to work with peers necessitates the hiring of more teachers to fill in normal workday gaps. To the extent that class size may be reduced in order to reduce the work loads of teachers taking on management responsibilities, more classes will be needed, and this too will entail greater costs. There is very little evidence, moreover, that student learning decreases as class size increases within the ranges that are being discussed in American schools today.

A Nation at Risk (National Commission for Excellence in Education, 1983) was sharply critical of how American teachers are trained. Teachers' pedagogical training is considered by most to have little academic or intellectual rigor, and teaching itself lacks the core of technological knowledge that is the hallmark of other professions (Lanier & Little, 1986; Lortie, 1975). Teachers themselves tend to attach little value to their preparation and rely on experience instead. Across the country, higher standards for teachers are being urged. The Holmes Group (1986), an organization made up of deans of schools of education, for example, recommends replacing the four-year undergraduate degree in education with a liberal arts degree in a chosen field followed by a year of graduate study in education. Few would argue with such suggestions. As we increase standards, however, we should remember that we might reduce the size of the pool of education candidates, particularly if one of the traditional attractions has been easy entry into the field. Although the state of California has for decades had a "fifth-year" program for teacher training, it remains unclear whether the quality of teachers in California is measurably higher than that in other states.

Lanier and Little (1986) have asked why teacher education is not better than it is. They point to its three major components — course work in general liberal arts studies, course work in specific fields of study (i.e., a major/minor), and course work in pedagogical study. Thus, there is what should be a shared responsibility throughout the university for teaching teachers, but no one is taking full responsibility. Professors in the arts and sciences risk a loss of academic respect if they take too much responsibility for or interest in teacher education. And those who do assume responsibility for teaching and supervising prospective and practicing teachers typically occupy the bottom of the academic ladder. The faculty in the leading graduate schools of education typically seek to "distance themselves from the confused and unattractive world of teacher education" (Judge, 1982, p. 9).

Today most university presidents urge their faculties to demonstrate a greater concern for the preparation of K-12 teachers. Unless the incentive and reward system within institutions of higher education changes, however, their urgings and those of others will have little effect. The issue comes down to this: Is the problem one of teacher training, or is it one of the quality and the life preparation of those who enter? To elaborate, would we rather have a very bright, motivated person who is well trained either in a discipline (especially germane for high school teachers) or in the art and science of handling children (especially relevant for K-6 teachers), or should we concern ourselves only with the new recruit's *potential* for becoming an exemplary educator if provided with the appropriate high-quality professional training?

Finally, any discussion of teacher training must extend to professional development experiences once a person becomes a teacher. There has been considerable discussion of (a) the role and effectiveness of supervising teachers once in the classroom, and (b) the opportunities for staying current with developments in the profession once prospective teachers have finished their preservice training. Though ongoing supervision and professional development are clearly desirable goals, we must recognize that such experiences are costly and likely require trade-offs against salary increases.

In this economist's view, the problem of attracting and retaining high-quality teachers is a problem of resources. It is largely an economic problem. We are laboring to attract more and better people to teaching at a time when the budgets of most public agencies are contracting due to both the transitory impact of a recession and the dramatically changing attitudes of voters, who consistently reject tax increases and bond issues for schools. Virtually all promising suggestions for attracting topflight people into teaching will cost money; consequently, new efforts on one front will likely cause diminished funds for and efforts on another. We must discuss and consider not the whole menu of possible procedures but rather those that will be most effective for a given budget. Again, from an economist's perspective, I conclude that we have been too quick to dismiss the possible benefits of a salary schedule calibrated to teachers' effectiveness.

Since the life earnings of a teacher are likely to be substantially less than those of other professionals, in order to bring the rate of return on the investment in becoming a teacher closer to the rates of return on investments in education for other professions, we must consider ways to reduce the cost of teacher training. One would scarcely be willing to incur a given cost of education if it were clear that later salary benefits were going to be fewer than in other professions. Such reluctance has several implications. First, policies advocating the extension of teacher preparation from four years to five or even six years often fail to consider that such a change will increase the cost and lower the rate of return from entering the profession. If such policies are to be implemented, it is vital that training costs be kept to a minimum. Scholarships and need-based aid must be provided for those seeking to enter the profession. Such aid will be even more effective if it covers not only out-of-pocket costs of tuition, but also some of the opportunity cost of staying in school for a fifth or sixth year. Also effective would be programs of loan forgiveness for teachers who remain in the profession for a set number of years. When a debt-laden college graduate has to choose among (a) going right to work in order to pay off loans immediately, (b) going to grad school in a field that will yield an income that will easily allow debt repayment, or (c) going into a graduate program that is just as expensive but will lead to substantially lower earnings, the choice is often clear. The feeling of doing good by helping children may be reward-ing, but not in all the right ways.

Teachers play a vital role in our society, and their contribution must be recognized and celebrated. The working conditions of many teachers are unconscionable and demand improvement. Unfortunately, most attempts to improve the status and working conditions of teachers cost money — a factor that in a time of dire budgetary conditions may make those attempts less realistic than they would otherwise be.

RESTRUCTURING

There is an important link between the issue of attracting top professionals into teaching and that of the restructuring of schools. To the extent that the class-room and the schoolhouse are congenial places for teachers to work, teaching will be seen as a proportionately attractive profession. Thus, as Dean Hentschke indi-cates in Chapter 9 of this volume, much of the discussion at the retreat on restructuring revolved around changes that will improve the working conditions of teachers. These include the use and misuse of time, the professional practices of teachers, authority relationships between teachers and principals, shared account-ability for student achievement, and the best use of outside contributions. A number of other potential restructuring ideas were not considered, presumably because they were viewed as unresponsive to teachers' needs. These included such issues as market-based or performance-based compensation systems, the elimination of tenure, peer review of teachers' performance, parental choice between public and private schools, and year-round schools. Though there is no question that any restructuring scheme should aim to increase the effectiveness of teachers, the issue of school restructuring *does* exceed the question of teachers' working conditions.

As Richard Elmore and his associates (1990) have pointed out, the major themes of restructuring have turned on empowerment, accountability, and academ-ic content. When discussing empowerment, however, we must ask: Empowerment of whom by whom? To whom are those newly empowered responsible? And how will a change in the structure of power affect established institutional roles, interests, and relationships among individuals at various levels? Schools are accountable now (for example, students are tested frequently and the results are published; commu-nity interests are often mobilized to affect course content, textbooks, and the like; federal and state governments issue mandates for special education students; vot-ers exercise choice over funding), but they are accountable to a very large number of interests, interests that are themselves splintered and often at odds. These con-flicts must be resolved if effective restructuring is to be achieved.

With regard to curricular content, Elmore et al. go on to point out that scholar-ly critiques of American schooling are remarkably unanimous on a single point: American schools do a poor job of imparting academic content. Advocates of reform claim that most teaching practices do not even approximate "teaching for understanding." To teach in this fashion, we need to change the way teachers themselves are taught, change the conditions under which they work, and change the relationship between research and practice. We may also need substantial changes in the curriculum. In sum, restructuring revolves around three imperatives: Teaching must promote understanding and problem solving, power must be shifted toward the schools and those whom they employ, and educators must be accountable to their clients and to the public generally.

Several routes to these goals have been suggested. First, we must change the modes of teaching and learning. We must reform the core technology of schools, a shift that can be effected through the cooperation of researchers and community and educational practitioners. The occupational norms of educators will have to be changed as well. These include licensure, school structure, working conditions, and the decision-making processes within schools. It was on the need for reforming teaching conditions that retreat participants focused their attention, and such reforms will have to be controlled by the educators in the schools. Finally, it has been suggested that the distribution of power between schools and their constituencies — or the governance structures that the schools operate — will need revision as well. In this, parents, students, and the public at large will have a major voice. Although political support for restructuring is broad, it may be too diffuse to support implementation of specific changes. Therefore, if school restructuring is to bè effective, reformers will have to negotiate the tensions likely to be stirred up among the various groups in question.

Changes in the technology of schools or in the occupational norms of educators empower those with expertise, whereas the client model empowers parents. Parents and educators will inevitably disagree over both content and pedagogy. Moreover, some schools that undergo restructuring will achieve greater gains than others. Empowerment does not guarantee equal results — a fact that may create serious inequalities among schools — and administrators will have to develop new ways of handling diversity and variability in school systems.

Debate over the issue of time illustrates a number of these potential conflicts. Educators at the retreat indicated that students should spend more time in school, both with and without the presence of teachers. They also argued for dispensing with schools' traditional (and ironclad) daily and annual schedules. Certainly parents concerned with child care both before and after school would concur with the extension of the school day. If supervision other than teachers' is required during nonclass time, however, the extra cost *will* have to be met; given current budget constraints, this may be difficult. Retreat participants also indicated that teachers require more time to teach, just as students require more time to learn. There is an important literature, however, that draws a distinction between "seat time" and "engaged time." It is easier to add more minutes to the school day than it is to find ways to ensure that when they *are* in class, students are actually being taught and are actually learning.

The issue of year-round school is another point of contention. It is difficult to identify any other institution in the country whose plants operate for only 9 or 10 months of the year. As a general principle, full utilization of the educational enterprise over the course of the year would yield obvious efficiencies. If salary schedules are predicated on teachers' working only for 9 or 10 months, however, additional funds would be required to hire them for the full year. If schools were operating for the full 12 months, it might be possible to engage students in learning year-round. Most advocates of year-round schooling, however, seek to serve more students per year, with none of them having more days of schooling than they do now. Some year-round plans, in fact, yield fewer days per year per student.

Even were year-round operation to provide more school days, the arrangement might meet substantial opposition. Parents as well as teachers are accustomed to time off in the summer, and many organizations, such as summer camps, have come to rely upon students to fill jobs that are available only in the summer. Still others fear that the intense summer heat in many parts of the country, and a lack of air-conditioned classrooms, would reduce students' ability to learn. In short, then, though there may be certain advantages to year-round schooling in terms of economic efficiency of student access to classrooms, the issues of cost and the disparity of interests may impede such a reform.

There are many other problems to restructuring schools. While accountability may be acceptable in principle, for example, historically it has been enforced very loosely, if at all. When those made newly accountable are found wanting in some way, there may well be disagreement on methods of evaluation and accountability generally, to say nothing of the objectivity of those doing the accounting.

While schools exist presumably to promote student learning, they are, in fact, expected to do much more. Tensions may arise over interpretations of academic learning as defined by technical experts, professionals, and students; over the range of other functions schools are supposed to perform; and over the relationship of these functions to academic learning. Since decisions on restructuring will be made within established state and local government structures as well as within the governance structures of school districts, rooted political interests with competing aims are bound to clash, and the result may be that schools adopt the rhetoric but not the substance of school restructuring. The alignment of political interests required to produce change on the scale desired is inherently unstable.

The transformation desired by those seeking restructuring carries with it several conditions. First, a realignment according to a common understanding of state and local policies on curriculum, research, development, and professional education is necessary.

Second, a radical redefinition of teachers' work would require aligning teacher education programs, certification policies, collective bargaining agreements, and management practices.

Third, changes in the governance of school structures would require changes in state and local staffing policies, curriculum and testing policies, and training and support for school personnel, as well as a major outreach effort to parents.

Fourth, it is assumed that there is a corpus of teaching methods appropriate to curricular content and a "basic" school organization that, together, point to the "right" restructuring paths. Pedagogy, curriculum, and school organization are not areas in which there is universal agreement, and so the question continues to arise: Restructuring the schools toward what?

Fifth, restructuring assumes that resources (such as staff time and money) and authority are dedicated to change. Given today's budget constraints, the issue of resources is problematic. Restructuring, moreover, addresses giving authority to new constituencies, but it rarely considers from whom that authority must be withdrawn in order to free it up for transfer. Where rewards and status derive from authority, the reduction of someone else's authority is clearly a problem.

It is easy for teachers and school site administrators to recite litanies of the changes that would make life easier for them and schools more effective for their students. It is also easy to omit from such recitations other changes that, although potentially effective, might not appeal to these groups. Most of the changes, however, require additional resources, and some require withdrawing certain assets from certain professionals. Thus, what is needed is a long-term commitment to basic change. We need new political coalitions that support change enough to make sacrifices for it. New terms of accountability are also necessary if external controls on schools are to be relaxed in return for demonstrable high performance. It is this desire for high performance — for improved student achievement — that must unite potential adversaries in the school reform and restructuring movement. Each of us must evaluate the potential for such a conflation of interests.

ASSESSMENT

Retreat participants focused their discussion of educational assessment on the drawbacks of multiple-choice tests, the need for performance-based or "authentic" approaches to assessment, and the importance of involving teachers in the design and implementation of testing. All these issues are important components of any discussion of assessment today. As an economist, however, I tend to view these issues in the context of a cost-benefit ratio and to consider expenditures according to competing demands and limited resources. My brief review of current testing practices will be cast in these terms, and I will raise certain questions regarding the actual costs and benefits of these efforts.

What are the characteristics of a sound test? That is, what do we want our tests to do and how do we want them to do it? The answers vary according to educational constituencies. Students, parents, teachers, administrators, employers, policymakers, politicians, and taxpayers are all "consumers" of tests and of the information they provide. These constituencies have a variety of often competing interests. Teachers tend to be most interested, for example, in tests that will serve as instructional improvement tools. They hold that test results should inform the curriculum and improve pedagogical decisions, thus improving students' learning. Administrators, on the other hand, have a decided interest in testing programs that are efficient and affordable, that is, in programs that are appropriate for all or at least most students, but that will not require vast expenditures of time or money. Politicians for their part want a measure of how well tax dollars are being spent, and the public wants to know how well its schools are doing. In short, everyone wants the schools to be accountable. But how?

As William Bennett (1988) has put it:

> There can be no accountability without accurate information for evaluation. Principals have to know whether a teacher is teaching well, superintendents need reliable information on district attendance, drop-out rates and student achievement, governors and state legislatures need to know where and how well their education budgets are spent, and parents need ready access to student performance data when trying to determine which school has the best program for their children (p. 48).

To find the answers to these demands, however, the various constituencies have relied neither on the results of Ms. Dove's weekly current events quiz nor even on her students' final exam scores. Rather, in recent years, "testing" has become synonymous with large-scale, multiple-choice, machine-scorable educational measurement programs such as the National Assessment of Educational Progress (NAEP) or the Iowa Test of Basic Skills. These tests have proliferated principally because they are thought to be efficient and affordable. In other words, large numbers of students can be tested and the results known in a relatively short time for a relatively low cost. And the pattern that follows is this: Newspapers publish the test results and politicians and parents use these reports to determine the effectiveness of schools, and teachers' and administrators' competence is judged according to the educational progress, or lack thereof, indicated by the scores.

Some claim such information is appropriate as the basis for modifying educational programs. The tests offer neat formulation, to say the least — but does it work? Certainly not as well as we might expect. If it did, presumably U.S. student academic performance in the last 10 to 15 years would have improved significantly, when in fact student performance, despite minor gains, has generally remained flat. Are the tests, or the uses to which we put these tests, to blame?

The literature offers several explanations for these disappointing results. Some researchers argue that the tests are simply invalid. Others say that it isn't the tests that present a problem, but the sanctions or rewards attached to the tests. Still others hold that such tests can be of great educational value, providing the correct tests are used for the correct purposes. The only thing these arguments have in common is that all of them call for some new type of measurement. Let's examine the arguments.

John Jacob Cannell (1988) generated considerable controversy when he reported that a 1987 50-state survey had found that not a single state was below the norm at the elementary school level on any of the six major (nationally normed) tests that were commercially available. Some 90 percent of school districts in the United States claimed to score above average. As many as 70 percent of the students tested nationwide were told their test performances were above the national average. Cannell explains his results by pointing out that tests are renormed only every 8 to 10 years. Thus, currently tested students are not compared to each other but to a past "normed group." High current scores, Cannell suggests, may be the result of any or all of several things: The initial norming may have been inaccurate, teachers may be "teaching to the test," or publishers may be "dumbing down" the tests to make them more attractive to school districts seeking higher scores.

Gary Phillips and Chester Finn (1988) have their own interpretation of Cannell's results. They note first that test publishers do not use the most rigorous standards for national probability sampling. School districts pick national tests, moreover, that are best aligned to their own curricula, and so their students naturally do better than the normed group. Local test takers are also more motivated to do well than the students in the norming sample. Phillips and Finn note that since norms are not updated as often as they should be, the repeated use of the same test format allows students and teachers to become familiar with test objectives, yielding "practice effects" that misleadingly inflate students' scores. Finally, the normed sample of students and the general population are not necessarily comparable groups. Test takers may not include handicapped and special education students who are included in the normed sample.

The extent to which Cannell's cynical conclusions should be taken seriously may be debated, but at the very least we must be cautious in interpreting the results of nationally normed tests.

Many argue that the teaching-learning-testing process has been corrupted by the high stakes that have been assigned to test outcomes. As George Madaus argues, "When important things like graduation, promotion from grade to grade, teacher evaluation, school district certification and financial support — major aspects of accountability affecting teachers or administrators — depend directly on test scores, it corrupts the process you are trying to improve" (quoted in Brandt, 1989, p. 26).

Many studies have found, for example, that teachers determine how much time they will spend on a given issue according to the likelihood of that issue's turning up on a test (Madaus & Airasian, 1978). Linda Darling-Hammond and Arthur Wise (1985) have found, moreover, that even within the bounds of a test-driven curriculum teachers tend to ignore basic concepts in favor of teaching exact test content. Thus, the curriculum becomes test driven. Needless to say, an attitude of, if it is not on the test why teach it? will limit students' learning, undermine teachers' professionalism, and ultimately ruin our entire educational system.

Why then *has* testing become such a high-stakes process? The answer lies in the perceived need to make schools more accountable. Beginning in 1957 with the Russian launching of *Sputnik*, continuing through the 1983 publication of *A Nation at Risk*, and following through to the current dismal showing of U.S. students in math and science (vis-à-vis their foreign counterparts), Americans have progressively lost faith in their public schools. Policymakers and the public alike have wanted to know — Do our children know enough mathematics, English grammar, and history to graduate from high school? Is Ms. Dove sufficiently well versed in biology to teach it? How well are the students in Los Angeles doing in relation to students in California generally? High-stakes tests with publicly reported results have been the measure ultimately employed to answers these quite legitimate questions. In essence, there has been an assumption that if schools performing poorly are "embarrassed" by the exposure of their failure, they will change their ways and become more successful.

But how will they become more successful? If Madaus is correct, high stakes alone seem to ensure a "teaching to the test" mode of operation using a watered-down curriculum — clearly not a formula for excellence in education. The answer lies in matching tests to needs. Many educational measurement specialists and cognitive psychologists hold that tests can be constructed for use by teachers to improve their daily instructional decisions. These specialists argue that such tests should be an integral part of instruction aiming neither to predict nor to satisfy accountability demands. Individual student gain should be the primary purpose of such tests.

In recent years, there has been a movement toward measurement-driven instruction (MDI), which is said to have real promise for improving classroom instruction *and* learning. MDI uses high-stakes achievement tests to direct the instructional process. The idea is that the consequences associated with performance on the tests will force an institutional response, and the tests content will "drive" instruction (Airasian, 1988). But if classroom instruction is to be influenced by the tests' stakes, their standards and their content must have a kind of symbiotic relationship, and a significant impact can be expected only when stakes and standards are high. Additionally, there is an assumption that instruction is sufficiently developed so that capable teachers can ensure student achievement. This assumption may not hold up, however, for the teaching of so-called higher-order skills. To date, processes such as basic reasoning, critical thinking, and problem solving have eluded clear means of both instruction and testing. Some argue, in fact, that in the end, tests intended to measure achievement will measure ability instead (Airasian, 1988).

Thus, our answer may not lie with any single type of testing. According to Popham (1990), the three missions of testing are (a) to determine the academic level of the individual student, (b) to evaluate the program in question, and (c) to improve instruction. None of these missions is well served when a test created for one is used to evaluate another. As Popham himself puts it: "Different educational purposes require differing educational tests and differing uses of those tests" (p. 12).

The preceding discussion leads us back to the National Educator Award winners' recommendation that teachers themselves be allowed and even encouraged to become more involved in both the design and the execution of tests. Given the complexities that swirl about the issue of testing — confounding even the shrewdest testing experts — one wonders what useful advice classroom teachers might be able to add. Perhaps teachers are at a disadvantage with such sophisticated technicalities. Perhaps, on the other hand, it is precisely they who would know best whether or not their students are "getting" what is being presented. Once we leave the realm of paper-and-pencil tests for the higher plane of performance-based or "authentic" testing, it may very well be that classroom teachers are best equipped to document student achievement.

Once again, an economic analysis of the costs and benefits of testing must recognize the additional costs of new approaches to assessment. These costs include in-service training of teachers as well as substitutes for those teachers taken out of the classroom to assist with test development. Teachers are already heavily burdened, and to add another set of tasks to their work load could be disruptive to both teachers and their students. The development of the tests themselves will also be costly. Many large testing corporations are willing to incur the costs of developing tests that will be widely used. If tests are to be tailored to specific classroom needs, however, test makers will lose the advantage of volume sales and be more reluctant to pay for test development. Submitting to a variety of performance-based tests, moreover, will divert students from instruction even more.

Finally, no discussion of assessment would be complete without a look at competency testing for teachers. A substantial majority of states now require teachers to pass some kind of test prior to certification. Tests for recertification, for merit pay, and for entry into teacher preparation programs have also been introduced in some states. Although the range of skills necessary to be a good teacher is so varied and subtle as to be neither measurable nor testable, it is reasonable to expect that all elementary and secondary school teachers possess at least minimum competency in English and perhaps other subjects as well.

On the basis of results of the competency tests required of all practicing teachers in Texas (Solmon & Fagnano, 1991), and of reasonable assumptions about teacher competency and student performance, we found that the benefit (in terms of lifetime earnings) to students of having teachers whose competence had been measured and approved far outweighed the cost of the measure — that is, the test — itself. It is reasonable that the retreat participants would not have given much thought to teacher competency testing. In considering the entire group of people in the teaching profession today, however, the need to winnow out the bottom tier may be quite urgent.

Though teacher testing is an important aspect of school reform in the United States today, the use of testing as a mechanism for reward and punishment versus testing as a tool for instruction has yet to be determined. As testing is often limited to paper-and-pencil multiple-choice tests of one kind or another, educators are also correct in advocating a broader set of methodologies. These issues heavily influence views on assessment. Whether we support or oppose one type of test or another, we must recognize that testing procedures will be with us for a long time.

BUILDING LINKAGES

The preceding chapter, "Business and University Collaboration With the Schools," which I coauthored, covered the subject of business-school and university-school linkages in some depth, and I do not have much to add on that subject here. I will simply underscore a number of the more central points raised in Chapter 11 and update the situation facing schools as they attempt collaboration these days.

For collaboration to be successful, it must hold potential benefits for all participants. The benefits to the school may be as simple as having a program underwritten. Schools need outside resources in order to operate at anything but the most marginal levels today. Although we have wholeheartedly endorsed the increases in teacher salaries that have occurred in recent years, given limited budgets, other operating expenditures have had to be sacrificed in order to fund the salary increases. Hence, anything outside sources can provide to make up the shortfall should be gratefully received.

However, we must always ask: What's in it for those providing help for the schools? From the corporate perspective, the ultimate consideration is: How do collaborations with schools improve "the bottom line?" Or, as Milton Friedman (1970) long ago said, "It is the responsibility of corporations to increase profits." The problem is that many corporate benefits from collaboration — in the form of reduced dropout rates, higher student achievement, or an improved labor force — are long-term outcomes whose relationships to collaborative projects may be tenuous. As most corporate leaders in the United States are held accountable on a quarterly basis when they issue their profit statements, the problems with collaborations yielding only long-term benefits are obvious.

In essence, collaborative projects are what may be viewed as luxury goods from the perspective of the corporation. When corporate profits are high and rising, one way that corporate leaders have chosen to deploy them has been to increase charitable giving in general, and contributions of money and other resources to the schools in particular. Discussions of business-school collaborations reached their highest pitch in the mid- to late 1980s, in the midst of the longest growth period since the Great Depression. But the economy has slowed in recent years. It has been widely discussed that corporate contributions have fallen off along with growth and profits. Hence, the optimism of the preceding chapter and its references must be tempered.

In recessionary times, many schools have seen programs started on "soft" corporate money run out of funds. Some of these programs have been terminated because both corporate resources and discretionary funds in the school's own budget have dried up. When practitioners (and probably students and parents) have to learn and/or implement a whole new program, only to have it disappear when external sponsors can no longer afford to be "civic-minded," they become understandably skeptical.

Though one way to assess the effectiveness of a collaborative effort is to see whether it continues when outside sponsorship ends, a program that by all objective criteria should have been preserved will nevertheless contract or disappear when neither internal nor external funds are available. The cessation of programs begun through collaborative efforts should not be taken to imply that they don't deserve to continue.

Similar problems apply to school-university efforts. As state legislatures and boards of trustees attempt to halt the cost spiral in higher education, we are embarking upon a period of "no frills" in universities. Although the rhetoric of university leaders may suggest that working with elementary and secondary schools is vital to universities' missions and success, such collaborations clearly are discretionary budget items that will be among the first cut when they are forced to trim their costs.

Collaborative efforts between schools and corporations or universities may have less promise today than they had only a few years ago. Although teachers and administrators in elementary and secondary schools should clearly continue to work at developing successful collaborations, the likelihood of their success will follow the curve (that is, will increase or decrease with the fiscal health) of the general economy.

CONCLUSION

As we review suggestions for preparing the types of students we would like to see graduating from our nation's high schools, we must recognize that virtually all of these ideas require significant additional revenues for the schools. Yet, we are making our suggestions during a period of intense budgetary constraint, not only in the schools, but also in other sectors that might well provide funds for schools. It is imperative, then, that we do more than provide wish lists for changes in K-12 education. Rather, we must select those changes that will be most effective, particularly most cost-effective. In an era of cost limitations, we cannot do everything that has potential. It is hoped that the discussions provided in this book will be used as a sort of menu from which we can choose the most effective projects in particular circumstances.

We must recognize that some paths will yield greater success than others, and we can only hope to have more successes than failures in the effort to develop the graduates we want. Effective elementary and secondary schools are vital to the success of our economy, our nation, and our future. Prosperity in the United States will require not only better schools, however, but greater commitments from every sector of our nation. The burden must not be placed on our schools alone.

BIBLIOGRAPHY

Academy for Educational Development. (1985). *Teacher development in schools* (Report to the Ford Foundation). New York: Author.

Airasian, P. W. (1988). Measurement driven instruction: A closer look. *Educational Measurement Issues and Practice, 7*(4), 6-12.

Alkin, M. C., & Solmon, L. C. (1983). *The cost of evaluation.* Beverly Hills, CA: Sage.

Arax, M. (1986, March 20). Time for brotherhood. *Los Angeles Times,* pp. 1, 8.

Ascher, C. (1990, March). Testing students in urban schools: Current problems and new directions. ERIC Clearinghouse on Urban Education, Institute for Urban and Minority Education. *Urban Diversity Series, 100,* 21.

Association of Teacher Educators. (1991). *Restructuring the education of teachers* (Report of the Commission on the Education of Teachers into the 21st Century). Reston, VA: Author.

Baker, E. (1990). Testing: Back to the future. *Center for Academic Interinstitutional Programs Quarterly, 2*(4), 1.

Bennett, W. (1988, April). *American education: Making it work.* Washington, DC: U.S. Government Printing Office.

_____. (1991, March 21). *What do we want our graduates to be like?* Presentation to the Milken Family Foundation National Educator Awards Retreat, Los Angeles.

Boyer, E. L. (1983). *High school: A report on secondary education in America* (Report for the Carnegie Foundation for the Advancement of Teaching). New York: Harper & Row.

Brandt, R. S. (1989). On the misuse of testing: A conversation with George Madaus. *Educational Leadership, 46*(7), 26-29.

_____. (Ed.). (1990). Restructuring: What is it? [Special issue]. *Educational Leadership, 47*(7).

Broudy, H. S. (1980). What do professors of education profess? *Educational Forum, 44*(4), 441-451.

Business Roundtable. (1989). *Business means business about education.* New York: Author.

_____. (1990). *The business roundtable participants guide: A primer for business on education*. New York: Author.

Cannell, J. J. (1988). Nationally normed elementary achievement testing in America's public schools: How all 50 states are above the national average. *Educational Measurement: Issues and Practice, 7*(2), 5-9.

Carlson, R. (1989). *Restructuring schools*. Internal memorandum, Washington, DC, Public Schools.

Carnegie Forum on Education and the Economy. (1986). *A nation prepared: Teachers for the 21st century*. Washington, DC: Author.

Carnoy, M., & MacDonnell, J. (1990). School district restructuring in Santa Fe, New Mexico. *Educational Policy, 4*(1), 49-64.

Casanova, U. (1987). Ethnic and cultural differences. In V. Richardson-Koehler (Ed.), *Educator's handbook: A research perspective*. New York: Longman.

Cavazos, L. F. (1990). Teaching ethics in the public schools. *NASSP Bulletin, 74*(528), 1-5.

Chapman, J., & Boyd, W. L. (1986). Decentralization, evolution, and the school principal: Australian lessons on statewide educational reform. *Educational Administration Quarterly, 22*(4), 28-58.

Children's Defense Fund. (1991). *The state of America's Children 1991*. Washington, DC: Author.

Chubb, J. E. (1988, Winter). Why the current wave of school reform will fail. *The Public Interest, 90*, 28-49.

Chubb, J. E., & Moe, T. M. (1990). *Politics, markets, and America's schools*. Washington, DC: Brookings Institution.

Clifton, R. A., Perry, R. P., Parsonson, K., & Hryniuk, S. (1986). Effects of ethnicity and sex on teachers' expectations of junior high school students. *Sociology of Education, 1*, 58-67.

Coles, R. (1977). What about moral sensibility? *Today's Education, 66*(3), 40-44.

Coles, R., & Genevie, L. (1990, March). The moral life of America's school children. *Teacher Magazine*, pp. 43-49.

Cooper, B. S. (1989). Education reform in Britain. *Education Week, 9*(10), 32.

Corcoran, T. B. (1989). Restructuring education: A new vision at Hope Essential High School. In J. M. Rosow & R. Zager (Eds.), *Allies in educational reform*. San Francisco: Jossey-Bass.

Dade County Public Schools. (1989). *Renaissance in education*. Miami, FL: Author.

Darling-Hammond, L. (1984, July). *Beyond the commission reports: The coming crisis in teaching*. Santa Monica, CA: RAND Corporation.

Darling-Hammond, L., & Berry, B. (1988, March). *The evolution of teacher policy*. Santa Monica, CA: RAND Corporation.

Darling-Hammond, L., & Wise, A. E. (1985). Beyond standardization: State standards and school improvement. *Elementary School Journal, 85*, 315-336.

David, J. L. (1989). *Restructuring in progress: Lessons from pioneering districts*. Washington, DC: National Governors' Association.

_____. (1991, May). What it takes to restructure education. *Educational Leadership, 48*, 11-15.

David, J. L., Cohen, M., Honetschlager, D., & Traimon, S. (1990). *State actions to restructure schools: First steps*. Washington, DC: National Governors' Association.

Delattre, E. J. (1981). No empty heads, no hollow chests. *American Educator, 5*(2), 20-23.

Duhl, J. (1990). *Increasing minority access to higher education through school-college collaboration* (Report for the Pew Charitable Trust). Philadelphia: Pew Charitable Trust.

Edmonds, R. (1979). Effective schools for the urban poor. *Educational Leadership, 37*(1), 15-23.

Elmore, R. F. (1987). Reform and the culture of authority in schools. *Educational Administration Quarterly, 23*(4), 60-78.

Elmore, R. F., & Associates. (1990). *Restructuring schools: The next generation of educational reform.* San Francisco: Jossey-Bass.

Elmore, R. F., & McLaughlin, M. W. (1988, February). *Steady work: Policy, practice, and the reform of American education.* Santa Monica, CA: RAND Corporation.

Etzioni, A. (1977). Can schools teach kids values? *Today's Educator, 66*(3), 29.

Finn, C. E., Jr. (1991). *We must take charge: Our schools and our future.* New York: Free Press.

Frankel, M., & Stowe, P. (1987). *New teachers in the job market, 1987 update* (NCES 90-336). Washington, DC: National Center for Educational Statistics.

Friedman, M. (1970, September 13). A Friedman doctrine: The social responsibility of business is to increase profits. *New York Times Magazine*, pp. 32, 33, 122, 124, 126.

Freistritzer, C. E. (1883). *The making of a teacher: A report on teacher education and certification.* Washington, DC: National Center for Educational Information.

Fruchter, N. (1989). Rethinking school reform. *Social Policy, 20*(2), 16-25.

Gaudiani, C. L., & Burnett, D. G. (1985/86). Academic alliances: A new approach to school/college collaboration. *Current Issues in Higher Education, 1*(1), 1-31.

Gollnick, D. M., & Chinn, P. C. (1990). *Multicultural education in a pluralistic society* (3rd ed.). Columbus, OH: Merrill.

Goodenough, W. (1987). Multiculturalism as the normal human experience. In E. M. Eddy & W. L. Partridge (Ed.), *Applied anthropology in America* (2nd ed.). New York: Columbia University Press.

Haggstrom, G. W., & Gissner, D. W. (1988). *Assessing teacher supply and demand.* Santa Monica, CA: RAND Corporation.

Hall, T. P. (1991, April 29). *Civic and Character Values-in-School Act of 1991.* Presented to the U.S. House of Representatives.

Harris, E. L., & Hoyle, J. (1990). The pros and cons of teaching ethics in the public schools. *NASSP Bulletin, 74*(528), 17-24.

Higher Education Research Institute. (1982). *Final report of the Commission on the Higher Education of Minorities.* Los Angeles: Author.

Hodgkinson, H. L. (1986a). *California: The state and its educational system.* Washington, DC: Institute for Educational Leadership.

_____. (1986b). *Texas: The state and its educational system.* Washington, DC: Institute for Educational Leadership.

_____. (1987). *New York: The state and its educational system.* Washington, DC: Institute for Educational Leadership.

_____. (1988a). *Connecticut: The state and its educational system.* Washington, DC: Institute for Educational Leadership.

_____. (1988b). *Florida: The state and its educational system.* Washington, DC: Institute for Educational Leadership.

_____. (1989a). *Illinois: The state and its educational system.* Washington, DC: Institute for Educational Leadership.

_____. (1989b). *Michigan: The state and its educational system.* Washington, DC: Institute for Educational Leadership.

_____. (1989c). *Minnesota: The state and its educational system.* Washington, DC: Institute for Educational Leadership.

_____. (1989d). *The demography of the mid-Atlantic states and their educational system.* Philadelphia: RBS Research for Better Schools.

_____. (1989e). *The same client: The demographics of educational and service delivery systems.* Washington, DC: Institute for Educational Leadership.

Holmes Group Executive Board. (1986). *Tomorrow's teachers: A report of the Holmes Group.* East Lansing, MI: Author.

Honig, W. (1990). Teaching values belongs in our public schools. *NASSP Bulletin,* 74(528), 6-9.

Jaeger, R. M. (1989). Certification of student competence. In R. L. Linn (Ed.), *Educational measurement* (3rd ed.). New York: Macmillan.

Jensen, L. C., & Knight, R. S. (1981). *Moral education: Historical perspectives.* Washington, DC: University Press of America.

Judge, H. (1982). *American graduate schools of education: A view from abroad* (Report to the Ford Foundation). New York: Ford Foundation.

Kaeste, C. F. (1984). Moral education and common schools in America: A historical view. *Journal of Moral Education, 13*(2), 101-112.

Kidder, R. M. (1991). Ethics is not a luxury: It's essential to our survival. *Education Week, 10*(28), 30-33.

Kuhn, S. E. (1990, Spring). How business helps schools. *Fortune, pp.* 91-106.

Lanier, J. E., & Little, J. W. (1986). Research on teacher education. In M. C. Wittrock (Ed.), *The handbook of research on teaching* (3rd ed., pp. 527-569). New York: Macmillan.

Levine, A. (Ed.). (1989). *Shaping higher education's future: Demographic realities and opportunities 1990-2000.* San Francisco: Jossey-Bass.

_____. (1991, March 21). *The graduates we want: Who they are and how we get them.* Presentation to the Milken Family Foundation National Educator Awards Retreat, Los Angeles.

Levine, M. (Ed.). (1985). *The private sector in the public schools: Can it improve education?* Washington, DC: American Enterprise Institute for Public Policy.

Lickona, T. (1988a). Educating the moral child. *Principal, 68*(2), 6-10.

_____. (1988b). How parents and schools can work together to raise moral kids. *Educational Leadership, 45*(8), 36-38.

Lieberman, A. (Ed.). (1988). *Building a professional culture in schools.* New York: Teachers College Press.

Lieberman, A., & Miller, L. (1990). Restructuring schools: What matters and what works. *Phi Delta Kappan, 71*(10), 759-764.

Linn, R. L. (Ed.). (1989). *Educational measurement* (3rd ed.). New York: Macmillan.

Linn, R. L., Graue, M. E., & Sanders, N. M. (1990). Comparing state and district results to national norms: The validity of the claim that "everyone is above average." *Educational Measurement: Issues and Practice, 9*(3), 5-14.

Lomotey, K., & Swanson, A. D. (1990). Restructuring school governance: Learning from the experiences of rural and urban schools. In S. J. Jacobs & J. A. Conway (Eds.), *Educational leadership in the age of reform*. White Plains, NY: Longman.

Lortie, D. (1975). *Schoolteacher*. Chicago: University of Chicago Press.

Madaus, G. F. (1985). Test scores as administrative mechanism in educational policy. *Phi Delta Kappan, 66*(9), 611-617.

Madaus, G. F., & Airasian, P. (1978, May). *Measurement issues and consequences associated with minimum competency testing*. Paper presented at the National Consortium on Testing, New York.

Maeroff, G. I. (1988). *The empowerment of teachers*. New York: Teachers College Press.

Matute-Bianchi, M. E. (1986, November). Ethnic identities and patterns of school success and failure among Mexican-descent and Japanese-American students in a California high school: An ethnographic analysis. *American Journal of Education, 95*(1), 233-255.

McCarthey, S. J., & Peterson, P. L. (1989, March). *Teacher roles: Weaving new patterns in classroom practice and school organization*. Paper presented at the annual meeting of the American Educational Research Association, San Francisco.

McDonnell, L. M. (1989). *Restructuring American schools: The promise and the pitfalls*. New York: Teachers College, Columbia University, Institute on Education and the Economy (ERIC Document Reproduction Service No. ED 314 547).

McManus, J. (Ed.). (1990, Spring). Saving our schools [Special issue]. *Fortune*.

Meade, J. (1990, March). The moral life of America's school children. *Teacher Magazine*, pp. 39-41.

Metropolitan Life Insurance Company. (1989). *The Metropolitan Life survey of the American teacher 1989: Preparing schools for the 1990s*. New York: Author.

Murphy, J., & Evertson, C. (in press). *Restructuring schools: Capturing and assessing the phenomena*. New York: Teachers College Press.

National Center for Educational Statistics. (1989). *Educational partnerships in public elementary and secondary schools*. Washington, DC: U.S. Government Printing Office.

National Center on Education and the Economy. (1990, December). *Restructuring education*. Rochester, NY: National Alliance for Restructuring Education.

National Commission for Excellence in Education. (1983). *A nation at risk: The imperative for educational reform*. Washington, DC: U.S. Government Printing Office.

National Governors' Association, Education Task Force. (1990, July). *Educating America: State strategies for achieving national education goals*. Washington, DC: National Governors' Association.

Northeast-Midwest Institute. (Ed.). (1988). *Education incorporated: School-business cooperation for economic growth*. New York: Quorum.

Nyberg, D. (1990, Summer). Teaching values in school: The mirror and the lamp. *Teachers College Record*, pp. 595-611.

Oakes, J., & Lipton, M. (1990). *Making the best of schools*. New Haven, CT: Yale University Press.

Olsen, L., & Mullen, N. A. (1990). *Embracing diversity: Teachers' voices from California's classrooms*. San Francisco: California Tomorrow Immigrant Students Project.

Pennsylvania Association for Retarded Citizens v. Pennsylvania, 343 F. Supp. 279 (E.D. Pa. 1972).

Phillips, G. W., & Finn, C. E. (1988). The Lake Wobegon effect: A skeleton in the testing closet? *Educational Measurement: Issues and Practice, 7*(2), 10-11.

Plisko, V. W. (1983). *The condition of education, 1983 edition: Statistical report.* Washington, DC: U.S. Department of Education, National Center for Educational Statistics.

Popham, W. J. (1987). The merits of measurement-driven instruction. *Phi Delta Kappa, 68,* 679-682.

_____. (1990). *Modern educational measurement: A practitioner's perspective* (2nd ed.). Englewood Cliffs, NJ: Prentice-Hall.

Pritchard, I. (1988). Character education: Research prospects and problems. *American Journal of Education, 96*(4), 469-495.

Rallis, S. F. (1990). Professional teachers and restructured schools: Leadership challenges. In B. Mitchell & L. L. Cunningham (Eds.), *Educational leadership and changing contexts of families, communities, and schools.* Chicago: University of Chicago Press.

Ravitch, D. (1985). *The schools we deserve.* New York: Basic Books.

Ryan, K. (1986). The new moral education. *Phi Delta Kappan, 68*(4), 228-233.

Shanker, A. (1990). A proposal for using incentives to restructure our public schools. *Phi Delta Kappan, 71*(5), 344-357.

_____. (1991, January 6). Multicultural and global education: Values free. *The New York Times,* p. E7.

Shepard, L. A. (1989). Why we need better assessments. *Educational Leadership, 46*(7), 4-9.

_____. (1990). Inflated test score gains: Is the problem old norms or teaching the test. *Educational Measurement: Issues and Practice, 9*(3), 15-23.

Sirotnik, K. A., & Goodlad, J. I. (Eds.). (1988). *School-university partnerships in action.* New York: Teachers College Press.

Sizer, T. R. (1984). *Horace's compromise: The dilemma of the American high school.* Boston: Houghton-Mifflin.

_____. (1990, March). Performances and exhibitions: The demonstration of mastery. *Horace,* pp. 1-2.

Sleeter, C. E., & Grant, C. A. (1988). *Making choices for multicultural education: Five approaches to race, class, and gender.* Columbus, OH: Merrill.

Smylie, M. A., & Denny, J. W. (1989). Teacher leadership: Tensions and ambiguities in organization perspectives. *Educational Administration, 26*(3), 235-259.

Sobol, T. (1990). Understanding diversity. *Educational Leadership, 48*(1), 27-30

Solmon, L. C. (1990). *A corporate manifesto for school improvement.* Unpublished manuscript.

Solmon, L. C., & Fagnano, C. L. (1991). Speculations on the benefits of large scale teacher assessment programs, or how 78 million dollars can be considered a mere pittance. *Journal of Educational Finance, 16*(1), 21-36.

Suzuki, B. H. (1990). *Multi-cultural education: The fad that won't go away and why it's now being taken seriously.* Paper presented at the National Association of Independent Schools Summer Workshop on Multicultural Education, Philadelphia.

Timpane, P. M., & McNeill, L. M. (1991). *Business impact on education and child development reform* (Study prepared for the Committee for Economic Development). New York: Committee for Economic Development.

U.S. Bureau of the Census. (1990). *Statistical abstract of the United States, 1990* (110th ed.). Washington, DC: U.S. Government Printing Office.

Weick, K. E. (1984). Small wins: Redefining the scale of social problems. *American Psychologist, 39*(1), 40-49.

Wiggins, G. (1989). A true test: Toward more authentic and equitable assessment. *Phi Delta Kappan, 70*(9), 703-713.

Wilbur, F. P. (1981). High school-college partnerships can work. *Educational Record, 62*(2), 38-44.

Wilkerson, M. (1989, Summer). *The curriculum and cultural diversity.* Princeton: College Board, Office of Academic Affairs.

Wilson, S. M. (1990). The secret garden of teacher education. *Phi Delta Kappan, 72*(3), 204-209.

Wilson, W. J. (1987). *The truly disadvantaged.* Chicago: University of Chicago Press.

Wise, A. E., & Gendler, T. (1989). Rich schools, poor schools: The persistence of unequal education. *College Board Review, 151,* 12-27.

Wolf, D. P. (1989). Portfolio assessment: Sampling students' work. *Educational Leadership, 46*(7), 35-39.

Wyatt v. Stickney, 344 F. Supp. 373 (M.D. Ala. 1972).

INDEX

low-income students and, 68, 97
minorities and, 7, 11-12
College preparation, diverse students and, 63
Colleges:
multiculturalism and, 33
"no frills" in, 120
race relations and, 32-33
remedial courses and, 91, 93
Common good, teaching respect for, 53
Common heritage, 13, 31, 32-33
Common values, 100
Communication, 48, 60
Community:
diverse students and, 62
nurturing from, 101
responsibility to, 47
values and, 54-55, 101
Compassion, 46
Compensatory education, 104
Computer classes, 23, 48, 70
Computer donations, 93, 97
Concept development, 60
Condon, Jeanette, 37
Conflict resolution, 55
Congress, early childhood intervention and, 29
Connecticut, teacher retention and, 70-71
Constitution, 42
Continuous learning, creativity and, 34
Cooperative learning, 55, 62
Coping skills, 47
Corporations:
assessment programs and, 89
early childhood intervention and, 29
management expertise and, 96
profit concerns and, 119
school partnerships with, 3, 47-48, 91-98, 119-120
Cost-benefit analyses:
assessment and, 114, 118
planning time for teachers and, 109
teaching students, 101
school improvement and, 3

Country, loyalty to, 19
Creativity, 48
continuous learning and, 34
measuring, 85
teaching, 13, 60
Critical thinking, 46, 60
assessment of, 85, 117
definitions of, 13, 40
instructional materials for, 62
teaching, 34
Cultural bias, standardized testing and, 85
Cultural diversity, 13, 46, 54, 57-63, 102-105
Cultural holidays, 61, 62
Cultural literacy, 27
Cultural pluralism, 58
Cultural sensitivity:
noninstructional staff and, 62
teaching, 53
Culture:
common, 31
defined, 58
dominant, 58
Current events, 48
Curriculum:
academic content and, 111
arts program in, 49
classical, 7
core, 23
cultural diversity and, 57
elective system, 7
extra-academic, 101
internal logic and integrity and, 48
multicultural, 33, 60-61, 104-105
personalized approach, 38
preparation for life and, 21
rigorous, 23
school restructuring and, 111-112
seamless fabric approach, 61
separatist, 22
social, 61
standardized testing and, 85
teacher proof, 61, 65
test driven, 116, 117

ABOUT THE EDITORS AND CONTRIBUTORS

EDITORS

LEWIS C. SOLMON, an economist, is president of the Milken Institute for Job and Capital Formation in Los Angeles. Prior to assuming this position in July 1991, Dr. Solmon had been dean of the Graduate School of Education at the University of California, Los Angeles, for six years. He has served on the faculties of UCLA, City University of New York, and Purdue, and as an adviser to the World Bank, UNESCO, and various government agencies and universities. Author of two dozen books and monographs, Dr. Solmon has written on teacher testing programs, foreign students, demographics of higher education, and education and economic growth, to name only a few subjects. He received his doctorate in economics from the University of Chicago.

KATHERINE NOURI HUGHES is communications director of the Foundations of the Milken Families. She was previously an officer at the strategic communications firm of Robinson, Lake, Lerer & Montgomery in New York, and served at the American University in Cairo. She completed her undergraduate and graduate studies at Princeton University, where she received her master's degree in Near Eastern studies.

KEYNOTE SPEAKERS

ARTHUR LEVINE is chairman of the Institute of Educational Management and a member of the senior faculty of the Harvard Graduate School of Education. From 1982 to 1989, he was president of Bradford College in Massachusetts and before that, senior fellow at the Carnegie Foundation and Carnegie Council for Policy Studies in Higher Education. Currently executive editor of *Change* magazine, Dr. Levine is also author of numerous articles and books, including *When Dreams and Heroes Died: A Portrait of Today's College Student* (Jossey-Bass, 1980) and *A Quest for Common Learning* (1981, with Ernest L. Boyer), and coeditor of *Opportunity in Adversity* (1985, with Janice Green). Dr. Levine took his doctorate at State University of New York at Buffalo and has been awarded five honorary degrees.

WILLIAM J. BENNETT is a senior fellow at the Hudson Institute and a senior editor of *National Review* magazine. He served as director of the Office of National Drug Control Policy (as "drug czar") from March 1989 through November 1990, and before that he was secretary of education. In 1981 he was named by President Reagan as chairman of the National Endowment for the Humanities. Dr. Bennett holds a doctorate in political philosophy from the University of Texas and a law degree from Harvard University. He has written extensively on social and domestic issues, and is author of *Counting by Race: Equality From the Founding Fathers to Bakke and Weber* and *Our Children and Our Country: Improving America's Schools and Affirming the Common Culture*.

CONTRIBUTORS

EVE BITHER is commissioner of Maine's Department of Education. She has also served in Freeport as superintendent of public schools, and in Portland as assistant superintendent for secondary education and assistant principal of both a junior high and a high school. In 1985 Ms. Bither won a grant to institute classes in Chinese in the Portland public schools. Ms. Bither has also taught physics at the high school level. She received her master's in education from the University of Southern Maine.

CAROLYN L. ELLNER is dean of the Graduate School of Education at California State University, Northridge. A former professor in the Department of Secondary and Adult Education at California State University, Northridge, specializing in the areas of developing teacher leaders and the problems of the disadvantaged, Dr. Ellner has also served on California's Commission on Teacher Credentialing. She has published numerous scholarly articles. Dr. Ellner received her doctorate in education, administrative studies, from the University of California, Los Angeles.

NANCY MAGNUSSON FAGAN is dean of the Graduate School of Education and Psychology at Pepperdine University. She is also a clinical psychologist who has conducted research in drug and alcohol education, publishing in such periodicals as the *Journal of Medical Education, Journal of Alcohol and Drug Education, Journal of Studies of Alcohol,* and *Journal of Drug Issues.* Dr. Fagan earned her doctorate in clinical psychology from Washington State University.

CHERYL L. FAGNANO is a Vice President of the Milken Institute for Job and Capital Formation. Previously she served as executive assistant to Dr. Lewis C. Solmon in his capacity as dean of the Graduate School of Education at UCLA. She has coauthored several articles with Dr. Solmon on teacher testing programs and faculty hiring practices. Dr. Fagnano received her doctorate from the University of California, Los Angeles.

HARRY HANDLER is adjunct professor at the Graduate School of Education at University of California, Los Angeles, where he teaches courses in urban education, school organization, and evaluation. Prior to that position, he was superintendent of the Los Angeles Unified School District. Dr. Handler's affiliation with Los Angeles schools has spanned 35 years and has included roles as teacher, counselor, director of research, and various senior administrative posts. Dr. Handler received his doctorate in education from the University of Southern California.

GUILBERT C. HENTSCHKE has been dean of the School of Education at the University of Southern California since 1988. Prior to holding his current post, he was dean of the School of Education and Human Development at the University of Rochester in New York. While on leave from that position, Dr. Hentschke was director of the Center for Urban Education of the Chicago Public Schools. Author of the books *School Business Administration: A Comparative Perspective* and *Management Operations in Education*, Dr. Hentschke is researching school restructuring, urban school organization, and teacher professionalism. He earned his doctorate in education at Stanford University.

HENRY MAROCKIE, West Virginia state superintendent of schools, served for nearly a generation as Ohio County (West Virginia) superintendent prior to his current appointment. He serves on the Council of Chief State School Officers Committee on Learning Technologies, on the Governor's Cabinet on Children and Families, and on the Professional Development Center Board. Dr. Marockie received his doctorate in education administration from West Virginia University and a master's in guidance and counseling from West Virginia University.

ALLEN A. MORI is dean of the School of Education and professor in the Division of Special Education at California State University, Los Angeles. Earlier in his career, Dr. Mori was dean of the College of Education at Marshall University in Huntington, West Virginia, and professor of educational leadership in the cooperative doctorate program with West Virginia University. Dr. Mori is author/coauthor of seven textbooks, including *Teaching the Severely Mentally Retarded, Adapted Physical Education*, and *Teaching Secondary Students With Mild Learning and Behavior Problems*. He received his doctorate in special education from the University of Pittsburgh.

EUGENE PASLOV, Nevada's state superintendent of public instruction, previously held a number of administrative positions in Michigan, including director of curriculum, director of federal programs, and deputy superintendent of public instruction. He was also the first director of the Governor's Office of Job Training. He has served as a high school guidance counselor and assistant principal. Dr. Paslov received a master's degree from California State University at Long Beach, as well as a second master's and a doctorate from Columbia University.

CHARLES TOGUCHI, superintendent of the Hawaii State Department of Education, has extensive experience in state government, including holding a seat in the Hawaii State Senate from 1983 to 1987 and a seat in that state's House of Representatives from 1977 to 1982. He has also served as the Hawaii State Teachers Association's political action and legislative director. Mr. Toguchi received a master's in education from California State University at Long Beach.

MILKEN FAMILY FOUNDATION NATIONAL EDUCATOR AWARD RECIPIENTS 1987-1990

AWARD RECIPIENT	POSITION/SCHOOL	STATE	YEAR
Lea Albert	Principal *Kahuku High & Intermediate*	Hawaii	1990
Margaret Allan	Teacher *Greenville Jr. High School*	Illinois	1988
Roberta Ameen	Teacher *N.I.C.E. Community Schools*	Michigan	1990
Deborah S. Anderson	Assistant Principal *Christopher School*	Illinois	1989
Evelyn Mae Andrews	Teacher *Tualatin Elementary School*	Oregon	1990
Neil Anstead	Curriculum Coordinator *Magnet School*	California	1987**
Delia B. Armstrong-Busby	Principal *Mitchell High School*	Colorado	1990
James M. Aseltine	Principal *Irving Robbins Middle School*	Connecticut	1989
Ede Jane Ashworth	Teacher *Brooke High School*	W. Virginia	1990*
Alfred P. Balasco	Department Chairman *Smithfield High School*	Rhode Island	1990
James B. Barlow	Teacher *Aloha High School*	Oregon	1990*
Barrie Becker	Teacher *Kirby Center School*	California	1989
Patricia R. Bell	Teacher *Shepardson Elementary School*	Colorado	1989
Sharon Belshaw-Jones	Director Elementary Educ. *Mission San Jose High School*	California	1988**

John Blaydes	Principal *J. H. McGaugh Elementary School*	California	1988
Jewell Boutte	Principal *Crenshaw High School*	California	1988
Charles M. Bowen	Associate Director *Jefferson School*	Illinois	1988**
Paul W. Bowen	Teacher *Petersburg High School*	Alaska	1990
Sheila J. Bowens	Teacher *Hamel School*	Illinois	1990
William B. Branch	Teacher *Evanston Township High School*	Illinois	1990
Ronald E. Bright	Drama Center Coordinator *Castle High School*	Hawaii	1990
Cynthia Ann Broad	Teacher *L'Anse Creuse Public Schools*	Michigan	1990
Sharon D. Brock	Principal *Boynton Elementary School*	Georgia	1990*
James Bryn	Teacher *Sparks High School*	Nevada	1990
Linda Bunch	Teacher *Independence Valley Elem. School*	Nevada	1988**
Jean Burkus	Teacher *Amity Regional Jr. High School*	Connecticut	1989
Susan M. Burt	Librarian *Marlinton Middle School*	W. Virginia	1990
Janie Pressley Butts	Teacher *Flanders Elementary School*	Connecticut	1990
Joyce C. Carey	Teacher *Benjamin Franklin School*	Illinois	1989
Michael Cassity	Associate Director *1st Liberty Inst.-Geo Mason Univ.*	California	1988
Francis Chamberlain	Director of Instruction *Napa County Schools*	California	1987**
Phyllis Cheaney	Principal *Lincoln School*	Illinois	1989
Elizabeth Ann Clemons	Teacher *Independence Elementary School*	Illinois	1989
Dora M. Cline	Bilingual Coord./Teacher *Dillingham High School*	Alaska	1990*
Margaret Clinkscales	Teacher *High Horizons Magnet School*	Connecticut	1988*
Louise E. Coleman	Superintendent *Joliet Public Schools*	Illinois	1989
Christine J. Comins	Teacher *Pueblo County High School*	Colorado	1989
Jeannette N. Condon	Principal *Fort Fairfield Elementary School*	Maine	1990

Steve Connolly	Teacher *Cloverdale High School*	California	1987
Teresa A. Corpuz	Principal *Albany Middle School*	California	1987
Rose C. Cousar	Choral Director *Screven County High School*	Georgia	1990
Robert L. Cross	Principal *Century School District*	Illinois	1989
Mary Bernadette Curtiss	Teacher *Trumbull High School*	Connecticut	1990
Joan T. D'Agostino	Department Head *Mt. Desert Island High School*	Maine	1990*
Matsumi Janet Daijogo	Teacher *Marin County Day Elementary School*	California	1990
Eddie L. Davis	Principal *Weaver High School*	Connecticut	1990
Jeanne E. Dawson	Teacher *E. S. Rhodes School*	Rhode Island	1990
D. Teresa R. deGarcia	Teacher *University Hill Elementary School*	Colorado	1989
Francey Dennis	Principal *Silver Lake Elementary School*	Nevada	1989**
Richard P. DuFour	Principal *Prairie View High School*	Illinois	1988**
John Duncan	Principal *Elderberry Elementary School*	California	1989
Robert Darlington Dyer	Teacher *Sea Road School*	Maine	1990
Mike Edwards	Principal *Cimmaron Memorial High School*	Nevada	1988
Jaime Escalante	Teacher *Garfield High School*	California	1988**
Dorothy J. Felicetti	Principal *Wilson School*	Illinois	1990
Cheryl M. Fisher-Allen	International Studies *Gilbert Stuart Elementary School*	Rhode Island	1990
Anita R. Fisk	Principal *Pershing County High School*	Nevada	1988*
James P. Ford	Principal *Sheldon High School*	Oregon	1990
Malinda Frazier	Teacher *Lovelock Elementary School*	Nevada	1990
Janis T. Gabay	Teacher *Junipero Serra High School*	California	1990
Teresa M. Gallman	Teacher *Woodbine Elementary School*	Georgia	1990
Elizabeth Garand	Teacher *Northwest Middle School*	Connecticut	1988

Gaylon Louise Garner	Teacher *Ralph Metcalfe Magnet School*	Illinois	1988
Norma A. Garnett	Chairperson *Tollgate High School*	Rhode Island	1990*
Frank D. Gawle	Department Chair/Teacher *Enfield High School*	Connecticut	1990
Jenlane Gee	Teacher *Sipherd Elementary School*	California	1989
Janice M. Gehrman	Teacher *Wm. H. Brown School*	Illinois	1990
John Genasci	Principal *Sparks Middle School*	Nevada	1988
Sandra K. Gilletti-Hay	Director Federal Programs *Evans Elementary School*	Colorado	1990
Shirley J. Gillis	Teacher *Harbor School*	Connecticut	1989
Pamela Lesiak Granucci	Teacher *Darcey School*	Connecticut	1989
Patricia Grimmer	Teacher *Carbondale Community High School*	Illinois	1989
Gary Hack	Teacher *Previous: Del Campo High School*	California	1988**
Lynne M. Haeffele	Supervisor *Bloomington High School*	Illinois	1988
Thomas Edison Hall	Teacher *Colquitt County High School*	Georgia	1990
Tim Harvey	Principal *Wm. E. Fanning Elementary School*	California	1990
LeRoy Hay	Acting Superintendent *East Lyme Public Schools*	Connecticut	1988**
Grace A. Heacock	Teacher, Deceased *Rosamond Weller Elementary School*	Alaska	1990
Suzanne Lyn Henning	Teacher *Tanana City School*	Alaska	1990
Margarita C. Hernandez	Principal *Burton Elementary School*	Michigan	1990
James D. Hieftje	Principal *Fremont Public Schools*	Michigan	1990
Edward E. Hightower	Principal *Eunice Smith Elementary School*	Illinois	1988
Peter Hodges	Principal *Alicia Reyes Elementary School*	California	1989
Herb Holland	Teacher *Audubon Jr. High School*	California	1990
Fred R. Horlacher	Teacher *Reed High School*	Nevada	1989
Richard A. Hunsaker	Teacher *Belleville West High School*	Illinois	1990

John D. Hurley	Principal *Harlem Sr. High School*	Illinois	1990
Amy Ish	Mentor *El Gabilan School*	California	1989**
Ben Jimenez	Teacher *Garfield High School*	California	1989**
Mae C. Johnson	Principal *Monterey High School*	California	1987
Louise C. Jones	Principal *Geo. Washington Carver Elementary*	California	1990
Mark D. Jordan	Assistant Principal *Gompers Fine Arts Option School*	Illinois	1989
Edward C. Keller III	Teacher *Second Ward Elementary School*	W. Virginia	1990
Thomas G. Koenigsberger	Teacher *Jefferson High School*	Illinois	1988
Roberta K. Koss	Teacher *Redwood High School*	California	1990
William C. Langley	Principal *St. Viator School*	Nevada	1990
Mary Laycock	Teacher *Nueva Learning Center*	California	1989
Margaret Leeds	Assistant Principal *Beverly Hills High School*	California	1987
Richard F. Lindgren	Principal *Illing Jr. High School*	Connecticut	1988
Craig Lindvahl	Director *Teutopolis High School*	Illinois	1989
Jerry A. Linkinoggor	Principal *Clay County High School*	W. Virginia	1990
Simon C. Lopez	Principal *Rockwood Elementary School*	California	1987**
Robert L. Lowry	Principal *Fisher Middle School*	California	1989
Charles H. K. Lutgen	Principal *Woodland Park Middle School*	Colorado	1990
Patrick Scott Mara	Teacher *South High School*	Colorado	1990
Lucia Dolores Martinez	Principal *Bradford Elementary School*	Colorado	1989
Joseph C. Mattos	Principal *James H. Bean School*	Maine	1990
Gene McCallum	Consultant *Audubon Junior High School*	California	1987
Kevin M. McCann	Principal *Jamieson Elementary School*	Illinois	1990
Clyde A. McGrady	Principal *Staley Middle School*	Georgia	1990

Robert W. Mellette	Program Director *Betsy Ross Magnet School*	Connecticut	1988
Paul M. Mello	Teacher *Middletown High School*	Rhode Island	1990**
Valerie Lynn Mills	Teacher *Ypsilanti High School*	Michigan	1990*
Yvonne Sanders Minor	Principal *Walter H. Dyett School*	Illinois	1990
Jean Miyahira	Teacher *Waipahu High School*	Hawaii	1990*
Cynthia B. Montoya	Librarian *James Gibson Elementary School*	Nevada	1990
Cosetta E. Moore	Curriculum Specialist *LAUSD Elementary Education*	California	1989
Roger Morrissette	Teacher *Sedgewick Middle School*	Connecticut	1989
Norma Mota-Altman	Teacher *Emery Park School*	California	1990
Larry Eugene Moye	Teacher *Barrow High School*	Alaska	1990
Ralph M. Murakami	Principal *Lihikai School*	Hawaii	1990
Linda Gray Murray	Department Chair *Hyde Park Career Academy*	Illinois	1988
Darrell Richard Myers	Staff Dev. Resource Teacher *Winship Junior High School*	California	1989*
Lorna Mae Nagata	Assistant Principal *Baldwin Elementary School*	California	1988
Nena Nanfeldt	Principal *Nathan Hale School*	Connecticut	1988
Billy D. Nave	Teacher *River Valley Alternative School*	Maine	1990
Karen S. Nemetz	Principal *Mission Avenue Elementary School*	California	1989
Philip H. Ogata	Teacher *Boulder High School*	Colorado	1990
Mary L. Omberg	Teacher *Nyssa High School*	Oregon	1990
Stephen M. Parker	Principal *Joaquin Miller Jr High School*	California	1990
Judith Pavlak	Teacher *Channing Memorial Elem. School*	Illinois	1990
Steve Pellegrini	Teacher *Yerington High School*	Nevada	1990
Louise Pempek	Administrator *Putnam Public Schools*	Connecticut	1989**
Phillip Perez	Director of Curriculum *Revere Elementary School*	California	1988

Wayne Piercy	Principal *Polytechnic Senior High School*	California	1990
Klaire B. Pirtle	Principal *Kingsbury Middle School*	Nevada	1988
Larry Ross Plew	Superintendent/Principal *Trinity High School*	California	1990
Linda Ann Poff	Teacher *Straley Elementary School*	W. Virginia	1990
Diane Price-Stone	Teacher *Philomath Elementary School*	Oregon	1990
John D. Putnam	Teacher *Washington Irving Jr. High School*	Colorado	1989*
Nelson W. Quinby III	Principal *Joel Barlow High School*	Connecticut	1989
Virginia Rebar	Principal *Haddam-Killingworth Middle School*	Connecticut	1990
Daniel J. Record	Teacher *Portland High School*	Connecticut	1990
Arthur Reisman	Teacher *East Leyden High School*	Illinois	1989*
Margaret Mary Reynolds	Teacher *Park View School*	Illinois	1990
Gayle A. Richter	Teacher/Department Chair *Zion Benton Tup High School*	Illinois	1989
Tom Ridgeway	Teacher *GA Academy for the Blind*	Georgia	1990
Doris Robertson	Director *Fulton County Schools*	Georgia	1990
Santra Truitt Robinson	Principal *M.L.K. Jr. Senior High School*	Michigan	1990
Pamela G. Rolfe	Teacher/Department Chair *Limestone Jr/Sr High School*	Maine	1990
Elaine Rosenfield	Teacher *Del Mar Elementary School*	California	1987
Shirley A. Rosenkranz	Teacher *Temple City High School*	California	1987
James H. Roth	Teacher *Riverwood Elementary School*	Illinois	1990
Patricia Rowe	Teacher *Lovelock Elementary School*	Nevada	1989
Kenneth R. Roy	Curriculum Director *Glastonbury Public Schools*	Connecticut	1989**
Donna W. Saiki	Principal *Hilo High School*	Hawaii	1990
Jennifer Jo Salls	Consultant *Nevada Department of Education*	Nevada	1989
Carol Ann Samsel	Teacher *Smalley Elementary School*	Connecticut	1990

Rhonda Buell Schier	Teacher *Ponderosa Elementary School*	Colorado	1989
Edward M. Schroeder	Teacher *Coolidge Jr High School*	Illinois	1988
Stewart R. Schultz	Teacher *West Bloomfield High School*	Michigan	1990
Rodolfo A. Serna	Assistant Superintendent *Chicago Public School District*	Illinois	1989**
Virgil Sestini	Teacher *Bonanza High School*	Nevada	1989**
Sylvia J. Shaina	Teacher *Thomas Edison Elementary School*	Michigan	1990
Doris Shipp	Teacher *Doris Reed Elementary School*	Nevada	1988
Robert Wilson Smith	Principal *South Kingstown Jr. High School*	Rhode Island	1990
Sanderson M. Smith	Teacher *Cate School*	California	1988
Dwight Souers	Teacher *Willamette High School*	Oregon	1990
Carol L. Sparks	Teacher *Foothill Middle School*	California	1987
Shirley Splittstoesser	Teacher *Wiley Elementary School*	Illinois	1990
Joan Steinberg	Teacher *Presidio Middle School*	California	1988**
Randal Steinheimer	Teacher *J.H. Freeman Elementary School*	Illinois	1988
Vivian Mallory Stephens	Teacher *Clairemont Elementary School*	Georgia	1990
Floyd Sucher	Principal *Chugiak Elementary School*	Alaska	1990
Marie Z. Sullivan	Teacher *Sabin Jr. High School*	Colorado	1990
Thomas Sullivan	Teacher *John Winthrop Jr High School*	Connecticut	1988**
Jeffrey R. Swenerton	Principal *Del Mar Hills Elementary School*	California	1987
Wayne Tanaka	Principal *Del Robison Jr. High School*	Nevada	1989**
Harold A. Taylor	Teacher *Lincoln Early Elementary School*	Michigan	1990
Jean C. Tello	Teacher *Amos Alonzo Staff High School*	Illinois	1988
Jane F. Thompson	Principal *Palisades Middle School*	Illinois	1988
Yvonne H. C. Toma	Teacher *Kipapa Elementary School*	Hawaii	1990

Nancy Lee Toupal	Teacher *East Street School*	Colorado	1990
Linda Bates Transou	Principal *Manual High School*	Colorado	1989
Joan Carole Turner	Teacher *Ruby Thomas Elementary School*	Nevada	1990
Phyllis Turner	Teacher *James Monroe Elementary School*	California	1990
Susan Van Zant	Principal *Pomerado Elementary School*	California	1989
David Vigilante	Teacher *Gompers Secondary School*	California	1988
Sidney E. Weathermon	Teacher *Martin Park Elementary School*	Colorado	1990
Carol R. Wheeler	Principal *Jack Jackter Elementary School*	Connecticut	1990
Marilyn Jachetti Whirry	Teacher *Mira Costa High School*	California	1988
Debra White-Hunt	Teacher *M.L.K. Jr Senior High School*	Michigan	1990
Lore H. Wiggins	Teacher/Department Chair *Gateway High School*	Colorado	1989
B. Eliot Wigginton	Teacher *Rabun County High School*	Georgia	1990
Virgil L. Wilkins	Teacher *Hundred High School*	W. Virginia	1990
Deborah G. Willard	Director *Glastonbury High School*	Connecticut	1988
Jean Carolyn Williams	Teacher *Douglas County Comp. High School*	Georgia	1990
Wilton Wong	Teacher/Department Chair *Jefferson High School*	California	1990

* Advisory Board Member

** Did Not Attend Retreat